privilege
~~privitedge~~
based upon context } ACADEMIC FREEDOM:
THE GLOBAL CHALLENGE ,

↑

academic freedom:
• testing of ideas | internal functions & external relations
• teaching
• research | • w/ nation-state

free expression:

↓

basic human right

"I don't have to change my mind, nor should my idea be challenged because it's my right to express my opinion"

Traditional views of academic freedom:

- ideas are tested at university
- pursuit of truth
↳ be willing to have your ideas tested
w/in your academic discipline or field

modern view of academic freedom

- help the public understand why the ideas you discovered help society move forward
↳ INTERACT W/ THE SOCIETY
be accessible

institutional autonomy: allow professors the responsibility of testing ideas & that progress is made towards truth
↳ protect the academy from government interference

ACADEMIC FREEDOM:
THE GLOBAL CHALLENGE

EDITED BY
Michael Ignatieff • Stefan Roch

CEU PRESS | CENTRAL EUROPEAN UNIVERSITY

© 2018 Michael Ignatieff and Stefan Roch

Published in 2018 by

Central European University Press

Nádor utca 11, H-1051 Budapest, Hungary
Tel: +36-1-327-3138 or 327-3000
Fax: +36-1-327-3183
E-mail: ceupress@press.ceu.edu
Website: www.ceupress.com

224 West 57th Street, New York NY 10019, USA
E-mail: meszarosa@press.ceu.edu

ISBN 978-963-3862-339

A CIP catalog record for this book is available upon request.

Printed in Hungary

Contents

Acknowledgements

We would like to express our gratitude to all the speakers and discussants at our academic freedom conference who have also contributed to this volume. We are grateful for their inspiring talks as well as their dedicated cooperation during the editorial process. We would like to thank Matyas Szabo, Kinga Pall, Ildiko Moran and Zsolt Ilija for their invaluable work in making the conference the success it was. We would like to thank Adri Bruckner and Peter Lorenz from the CEU Communications Department for their editorial support in putting this volume together. Finally, we would like to express our gratitude to Linda Kunos and Krisztina Kós from CEU Press for their wonderful cooperation in producing this publication.

Michael Ignatieff
Stefan Roch

Academic Freedom From Without and Within
—— *Michael Ignatieff*

—— Michael Ignatieff is President and Rector of Central European University

I

In June 2017, CEU convened a gathering of international experts and political figures to examine the state of academic freedom world-wide. This volume summarizes the highlights of our discussions. We ranged widely, from the closing of universities in Turkey and the narrowing space for academic freedom in Hungary, China and Russia, to the controversies about free speech roiling American campuses. In this volume, you will read thoughtful historical analysis of the origins of the ideal of academic freedom; eloquent testimony from the front lines of the battle to defend the academy as a free space for controversial thought; as well as analysis of how university autonomy and self-government are endangered by hostile political forces around the world. We hope students and faculty, university administrators, journalists and politicians in many countries will find our CEU discussion a useful guide in understanding the global nature of the challenge to academic freedom.

If there is a single conclusion from this volume it is that academic freedom is too important to be left to universities to defend by themselves. Universities need to rebuild public confidence in their mission.

These days higher education is politically isolated: attacked as bastions of elite privilege and castigated as the protected domain of arrogant experts. Universities cannot afford to let populist political forces turn these feelings to their own electoral benefit. Universities need to stand up for themselves and take their case to the public. Free universities are critical to the survival of democracy itself. Free institutions nourish free thought and free thought winnows the kernel of knowledge from the chaff of falsehood. Without knowledge, based in patient verification and self-questioning, democracies are flying blind. At a time when the authority of knowledge in public debate is questioned as never before, universities need to stand up for their role as critical custodians of what societies, through experimentation and trial and error, actually know.

Central European University has been defending the principle of academic freedom and institutional autonomy throughout its twenty-six-year history in Budapest. In 2017, our dispute with the Hungarian government over whether we could remain in Budapest became a global *cause celebre*. More than 500 prominent US and European academics, including more than twenty Nobel Laureates, signed an open letter to support CEU. Political leaders across Europe have voiced their support and thousands marched in the streets of Budapest in defense of CEU and academic freedom.

CEU's struggle is not over, but the story is worth summarizing briefly because of the light it sheds on the pressures that academic freedom faces even in nominally democratic societies in the 21st century. In March 2017, the government passed a law in Parliament changing the regulations governing foreign educational institutions operating in Hungary. Normally an elected government consults with institutions before they initiate important legal changes. No consultation occurred before the law was tabled in Parliament. Normally a law's application is universal. It should apply to all. This was not the case in Hungary. The law that has come to be known as 'lex CEU' singled out CEU directly: it forbade us to maintain our dual Hungarian and American legal identity and required us to choose either a Hungarian or American accreditation; it required us to have a campus in the United States, when we are among nearly 30 US institutions overseas who do not maintain a campus in the US. Lex CEU also required our non-European staff to secure work permits, despite the fact that we had an exemption from this requirement for many years. Finally, our legal status in Hungary was made to depend on a new bilateral agreement between Hungary and the state in which we originate. At first the Hungarian government insisted that such an agreement should be with the United States. The US government pointed out that the US constitution leaves jurisdiction in matters of higher education to the states. Eventually, in order to break the impasse, the Governor of New York State, where we are accredited, offered to negotiate a new agreement with Hungary to settle CEU's legal status once and for all. Through the summer of 2017, the negotiations made good progress. A text of the agreement was finalized in September that would allow CEU to remain in Budapest. CEU agreed a further agreement with Bard College to conduct educational activities in New York. In October, in a sudden reversal, the Hungarian government decided not to sign the New York deal and instead to extend the deadline for compliance with the original lex CEU for another year.

Until January 2019, CEU remains in legal limbo, free to admit new students, but uncertain of its legal status in Hungary thereafter. Speculation about the government's motives or its ultimate intentions is pointless. What is clear is that the university's legal situation is a telling illustration of the difference between 'rule by law' and 'rule of law', between arbitrary political discretion and lawful certainty. Just as rule of law is essential for democracy, so rule of law is critical for any academic freedom worth having.

Even if Hungary were to eventually decide that we are not in compliance with lex CEU—CEU's position is that we are—CEU's existence is not threatened. The difficulty we have experienced is not an existential crisis. CEU has the resources and the reputation to continue its degree programs uninterrupted whatever happens next. Other universities around the world, harassed by their governments or by hostile political forces, may not be so lucky. At CEU itself, life goes on. Our classes are full, our faculty continues their research, and we are in the middle of a strategic planning process that will set the course for the university's development through the year 2022.

II

CEU's experience may be unique in the history of European higher education in recent times, but in a wider context, it is not exceptional. Many other universities around the world face much more serious threats to their institutional and legal autonomy. In Turkey, public universities have been closed; faculties have been dismissed en masse; the purge of students continues more than a year after the Turkish coup and counter-coup. In St. Petersburg, the European University of St. Petersburg struggles to stay alive in the face of recurrent official challenges to its legal status. In China, the Communist Party has re-imposed ideological discipline on universities and colleges, after a brief period of liberalization, and the space for free thought and free expression has narrowed. Foreign universities operating in China have had to adjust to new restrictions that limit free collaboration with other Chinese institutions.

In defending academic freedom against these threats, international universities, who have pioneered the globalization of higher education, need to develop shared rules about how to work in authoritarian and semi-authoritarian contexts and to stand up for each other when these rules are broken. Certainly, CEU benefited enormously from the support we received from the international academic community.

At the same time as authoritarian and semi-authoritarian governments are restricting or abolishing academic freedom, there are threats to academic freedom in well-established democracies as well.

Freedom is being undermined by forces outside the academy, but also by partisan political passions within. Political space is polarizing everywhere, and universities themselves are no exception. Some professors and students appear to believe that academic freedom is valuable only to the extent that it enables them to promote one set of political opinions while banishing others. In the United States, at Middlebury College a crowd shouted down a conservative author and left a professor who came to his aid with a concussion; in Oregon, a professor was harassed for refusing to join a protest against racism. In Berlin and in Dresden, professors have been bullied for conservative views or for attempting to explain the appeal of the extreme far right. A university that becomes a safe haven only for liberal or progressive views is betraying the cause of academic freedom itself.

This is one reason why universities have forfeited some public support and why coded attacks on 'political correctness' on campus have secured a wide hearing at least in the United States.

Far away from university seminar rooms, research labs and libraries, many people have been persuaded, by politicians and media alike, to regard academic freedom as the questionable privilege of a tenured elite. In publicly funded universities, professors' salaries are paid for by citizens who may have never had the chance at a post-secondary education. Resentment at the privileges of academic life, such as they are, is widespread.

What can be done to strengthen public support for academic freedom? The answer may lie in rebalancing the relation between academic freedom and social responsibility. Scholars, researchers and teachers need freedom to think and learn, but in return they need to communicate their research to their fellow citizens and, wherever possible, make their teaching and learning useful to the societies they serve. Universities need to do everything they can to remove barriers—economic, cultural and

CEU students and staff saying thank you to all supporters

psychological—that deny fellow citizens the chance to secure a college or university education. The privileges of academic freedom come with responsibilities to our societies and communities which we need to discharge as best we can.

In order to strengthen public support for academic freedom, we also need to get out the message that our freedom protects theirs. At the moment, this message is not being heard. If you ask people on the street what academic freedom means, some will say it means professors have a job for life. In a world of pervasive economic insecurity, the privileges

of the tenured few look hard to justify. We need to remind the public that tenure protects them too, by defending the right to pursue unpopular research and take unpopular positions. It is one of the counter-majoritarian bulwarks of a free society, like a free press or an independent judiciary.

Academic freedom is also commonly attacked as a license for arrogant academic expertise. The popular dislike of 'expertise' has been exploited by populist politicians who pit 'the people', against a credentialed minority. University leaders need to say clearly that our societies would descend into blind chaos without academic knowledge, without evidence-based public policy and the rigorous testing, by universities, of political ideas and their implementation.

The deeper problem is an erosion of the connection between academic freedom and the freedom of all citizens. The number of our fellow citizens who will say "academic freedom is my freedom too" are in a minority.

Universities need to make the case that democracy includes the right of institutions, not just universities, to govern themselves free of outside interference. Unless institutions can defend their right to govern themselves against outside forces—and this may include both governments and pressures from corporate interests and donors—they cannot effectively defend the rights of their members within and they cannot speak up for citizens outside their walls.

A strong democracy requires institutions sufficiently independent to counter-balance majority rule, to defend minority opinions and minority rights. Universities belong with the courts, the media, professional associations and civil society organizations as critical defenders of a democracy robust enough to resist the drift to tyranny.

When democracies are weak, when rule of law, checks and balances, freedom of the press and an independent judiciary are eroded, universities become vulnerable. Universities have a visceral interest in doing what they can, with their teaching and research, to strengthen respect for the democratic institutions on which their own freedom depends.

Democracy is, above all, the noble ideal of free communities choosing their aims for themselves, giving themselves rules by consent, and discharging obligations of protection and care to their members. Where did this ideal first take root in Europe? In the community of scholars, in the medieval universities of Bologna, Salamanca, Oxford, Cambridge, the Sorbonne, Heidelberg, and the great early modern universities of eastern Europe, the Charles University in Prague, Jagiellonian in Cracow, or Eötvös Loránd in Budapest: all founded centuries ago, all still governing themselves, all the kernel of an ideal of self-rule that is the very core of the democratic faith. Academic freedom, therefore, is one of democracy's ancestors and today it has become one of its vital conditions.

Academic Freedom: The Tension Between the University and the State —— *Joan Wallach Scott*

—— *Joan Wallach Scott is professor emerita in the School of Social Science at the Institute for Advanced Study in Princeton, New Jersey. She is a long-standing member of the Committee on Academic Freedom and Tenure of the American Association of University Professors (AAUP).*

Academic freedom is highly specific to institutions of scholarly research and teaching; it is not, like liberty or equality, a universal human right. It is not a general right of free speech, although the two are often confused. Instead, academic freedom applies to those of us who are associated with universities. It refers both to the internal functions of the university—to the research and teaching that go on here—and to the external relations of the university with the nation-state.

It is the question of the relationship between the university and the state that I want to address today. The relationship is not a simple one; it is traversed by tensions that are necessary and unresolvable. I will look at two of these tensions. The first is between the search for truth and the demands of power, what might be called a tension between *raison* and *raison d'état*. The second tension is between the hierarchical structure of the academy and the principles and practices of political democracies. I will argue that academic freedom mediates both of these tensions.

The University and the Nation

The origin of the modern university has everything to do with nation-building. An older history is that of the religious sponsorship of universities, with the various relations between churches and states affecting their governance. Medieval universities were established to train priests, lawyers, doctors and schoolmasters, not always with state sanction. It was Wilhelm von Humboldt who provided the model for the modern university at the University of Berlin early in the 19th century. One scholar has described its function this way: the Humboldtian university, he writes, "[is] the institution charged with watching over the spiritual life of the people of the rational state, reconciling ethnic tradition and statist rationality."[1] In Humboldt's vision, shared by many of his German Idealist colleagues, the university's mission was to produce students committed to discovery and to inculcate the common language, history, literature, and geography that made possible the creation of a shared national culture. This unifying culture served not only a domestic function, but became an important arm of international competition and imperial expansion. From the late 18th century on, there has been a tension between two avowed purposes of the university: to educate the citizens of the nation-state and, equally importantly, to encourage the critical thinking that would correct abuses of power and furnish the nation with the creativity and change that were vital to national well-being. Unfettered rational inquiry was taken to be the best guarantee of a healthy national future. This was Emmanuel Kant's argument in "The Conflict of the Faculties."[2] There Kant insisted that the faculty of philosophy (the so-called lower faculty) was the most vital arm of the university because its job was to interrogate the very foundations of the higher faculties of theology, medicine, and law. Philosophy's interrogation was a correction not only to stale disciplinary orthodoxy, but also to the dangers of unfettered state power and its

---

[1] Bill Readings, *The University in Ruins* (Cambridge: Harvard University Press, 1996), 15.
[2] *The Conflict of the Faculties (Der Streit Der Fakultäten)*, ed. Mary J Gregor (Lincoln: University of Nebraska Press, 1979).

influence on those more practical disciplines. Kant's essay captures the dilemma that faced the modern university: how to reconcile reason and the state, the search for truth and the requirements of power.[3] The literary scholar Masao Miyoshi described this dilemma as a tension between "utilitarian nationalism" (whose aim is to secure the national good) and "anti-utilitarian inquiry" (which depends on free and spontaneous expression). "The university as an institution has served Caesar and Mammon," he wrote, "all the while manifesting its fealty to Minerva, Clio, and the Muses."[4]

This tension at the heart of the university's mission has been apparent throughout its history, although changes in demography and curriculum in the nations of the West have sometimes made it less apparent. Neo-liberal transformations have certainly taken attention away from both national agendas and critical thinking: students are now more likely to be treated as paying clients, whose human capital can be enhanced by a university education and whose vocational interests should dictate the curriculum. The research and development needs of private companies more often drive the inquiries of professors (especially in the sciences), and globalization—not national interest—is at the heart of what some have termed "the information and knowledge industry."[5] Still, I would argue that the Humboldt model has not entirely disappeared; its tensions remain as a legacy to be drawn on.

Those tensions have been clearly evident in the post-colonial era, as new nations emerged to claim identities either denied or suppressed by imperial rule. Edward Said wrote compellingly of this process in a 1996 article on "Identity, Authority, and Freedom." There he pointed

---

[3] M. Miyoshi, "Ivory Tower in Escrow," *Boundary 2* 27, no. 1 (March 1, 2000): 58, doi:10.1215/01903659-27-1-7.
[4] Ibid., 13.
[5] Ibid.

out, referring to developments in the Middle East, that "Arab universities are not only nationalist universities, but are also political institutions for perfectly understandable reasons."[6] Understandable because "all societies accord a remarkable privilege to the university and school as crucibles for shaping national identity." Once national independence had freed these nations from the yokes of Ottoman or European imperialism, he noted, an opportunity opened to educate young people—to develop their pride—in the traditions, languages, history, and culture of their own countries. (The same might be said of the nations of Eastern and Central Europe after the end of Soviet rule in 1989.) But a terrible problem soon arose, Said noted, when national universities were "reconceived as extensions of the newly established national security state." As a result, the real value of education was short-circuited by the ruling party which sought "political conformity rather than intellectual excellence." "Nationalism in the university has come to represent not freedom but accommodation, not brilliance and daring but caution and fear, not the advancement of knowledge but self-preservation."[7] "Political repression," he went on, "has never been good for academic freedom, and, perhaps, more importantly, it has been disastrous for academic and intellectual excellence."[8] The two—academic freedom and intellectual excellence—are, of course, entirely interdependent.

Without wanting to deny the importance of education for the construction of national identity, Said asked: "which national identity?" and how might it be understood in relation to academic freedom? His answer—which I will quote at length because I cannot match its clarity and eloquence—acknowledges the needs of the nation, but makes critical intellectual work its own raison d'être. "My assessment of Arab academ-

[6] Edward W. Said, "Identity, Authority and Freedom: The Potentate and the Traveler," in *The Future of Academic Freedom*, ed. Louis Menand (Chicago: The University of Chicago Press, 1996), 218.
[7] Ibid., 219.
[8] Ibid., 220.

ic life is that too high a price has been paid in sustaining nationalist regimes that have allowed political passions and an ideology of conformity to dominate—perhaps even to swallow up—civil institutions such as the university. To make the practice of intellectual discourse dependent on conformity to a predetermined political ideology is to nullify intellect altogether."[9] For Said, intellectual discourse is above all, "the freedom to be critical: criticism *is* intellectual life and, while the academic precinct contains a great deal in it, its spirit is intellectual and critical, and neither reverential nor patriotic (...)" It is the freedom to critique the terms of an exclusionary national identity that is vital both to the university and the nation, "Otherwise, I fear, the old inequities, cruelties, and unthinking attachments that have so disfigured human history will be recycled by the academy, which then loses much of its real intellectual freedom as a result."[10] Here, in a somewhat different language, is Kant's idea that critical philosophy provides the ultimate corrective to abuses of state power.[11]

Said's notion of national identity was one that disclaimed the triumph of one people over another and the insistence on homogeneity as the bottom line of a common culture. Instead, it is the recognition—enabled by critical thinkers in the humanities and social sciences especially—of its relation to other national identities, and, within the nation, to the multiple identities we inhabit, to the differences that bind us, to a commonality of shared differences rather than to a genetic or historical sameness. Even more important was the lesson "that human life and history are secular—that is actually constructed and reproduced by men and women."[12] This means that there is nothing fixed about our social and political arrangements, that they are open to criticism and to change. It is precisely the specter of change, of course, that threatens the rulers of the authoritarian state.

---

[9] Ibid.
[10] Ibid., 223.
[11] Ibid., 220.
[12] Ibid., 223.

Said argued that the function of academic freedom was to protect and preserve the critical spirit, ensuring the pursuit of justice and truth wherever it might lead. "Rather than viewing the search for knowledge in the academy as the search for coercion and control over others, we should regard knowledge as something for which to *risk* identity, and we should think of academic freedom as an invitation to give up on identity in the hope of understanding and perhaps even assuming more than one."[13]

Academic Freedom

"Our model for academic freedom," Said wrote, "should be the migrant or traveler," voyaging beyond familiar places, confronting the unknown.[14] For him, academic freedom is a kind of passport for international travel—guaranteeing the right of scholars to go wherever the search for truth may lead. It was one way of addressing the tension at the heart of the mission of the modern university—that between utilitarian nationalism and non-utilitarian inquiry, between reason of state and reason itself.

In the United States, the concept of academic freedom was formulated by a group of professors at the turn of the last century, precisely as a way of mediating that tension, of providing a rationale for an autonomous faculty, not as a peculiar elitist privilege, but as a guarantee of advancing "the common good." In 1915, the newly organized American Association of University Professors (AAUP), among them the American pragmatist John Dewey, articulated a vision of the university that was at once immune to powerful interests (in the US these were both state legislators and private benefactors—Caesar and Mammon), and that promised to serve them, however indirectly, by producing new knowledge for the common good. Their version of academic freedom rested on the notion that knowledge and power were separable: the pursuit of truth ought to have nothing to do with public conflicts of interest, even if new knowledge could weigh

---

[13] Ibid., 227.
[14] Ibid.

in on one side or another of those conflicts. The university was defined as "an inviolable refuge from [the] tyranny [of public opinion] (...) an intellectual experiment station, where new ideas may germinate and where their fruit, though distasteful to the community as a whole, may be allowed to ripen."[15] As that last reference to "distasteful" reactions indicates, academic freedom was designed to protect the most critical, the most unorthodox of university faculty. A professor ought to be "a contagious center of intellectual enthusiasm," wrote one university president. "It is better for students to think about heresies than not to think at all; better for them to climb new trails and stumble over error if need be, than to ride forever in upholstered ease on the overcrowded highway."[16]

The best statement I have seen of the principle of academic freedom comes from the regents of the University of Wisconsin in 1894, repudiating efforts by state legislators to fire a professor because his teaching did not conform to their economic views.

> As Regents of a university with over a hundred instructors supported by nearly two millions of people who hold a vast diversity of views regarding the great questions which at present agitate the human mind, we could not for a moment think of recommending the dismissal or even the criticism of a teacher even if some of his opinions should, in some quarters, be regarded as visionary. Such a course would be equivalent to saying that no professor should teach anything which is not accepted by everybody as true. This would cut our curriculum down to very small proportions. We cannot for a moment believe that knowledge has reached its final goal, or that the present condition of society is perfect. We must therefore welcome from our teachers

[15] AAUP, "Declaration of Principles on Academic Freedom and Tenure," 1915, 32.
[16] Ibid., 36.

such discussions as shall suggest the means and prepare the way by which knowledge may be extended, present evils be removed and others prevented. We feel that we would be unworthy of the position we hold if we did not believe in progress in all departments of knowledge. In all lines of academic investigation it is of the utmost importance that the investigator should be absolutely free to follow the indications of truth wherever they may lead. Whatever may be the limitations which trammel inquiry elsewhere we believe the great state University of Wisconsin should ever encourage that continual and fearless sifting and winnowing by which alone the truth can be found.

1894 Ely trial committee final report[17]

The autonomy of professors, defended in this statement, rested on the fact that the faculty was a self-regulating body, trained and credentialed according to the rules of their discipline and profession. They were, in the words of the philosopher John Dewey, "an organized society of truth-seekers" uniquely qualified to judge one another's abilities. These organized societies were the national professional associations that trained and certified competence, a form of expertise we depend on for the advancement of knowledge in all fields. The legal scholar Robert Post puts it this way: "Disciplines are grounded on the premise that some ideas are better than others; disciplinary communities claim the prerogative to discriminate between competent and incompetent work."[18] University administrators (those charged with the efficient running of the institution and its legal and financial operations) and trustees (who govern with ultimate authority) are not in a position to question the exper-

---

[17] See: Theodore Herfurth, "Sifting and Winnowing: a Chapter in the History of Academic Freedom at the University of Wisconsin," 1949, 11.
[18] Robert Post, *The Classic First Amendment Tradition Under Stress: Freedom of Speech and the University* ([unpublished], 2017), 16.

tise of the faculty in matters of research and teaching; instead they share governance with the faculty, each carrying responsibility for separate activities, together ensuring the viability of the institution. The guarantee of academic freedom is at the heart of their relationship.

I was reminded as I wrote this of an experience I had here at CEU, more than 15 years ago, during the tumultuous reign of the Rector Yehuda El-kana. At one meeting that I attended, he confronted faculty and students who were protesting the planned reform or elimination of programs in gender studies and environmental studies. There he justified his right to decide unilaterally, with a phrase that was endlessly ridiculed by those who considered him something of a tyrant. "A university is not a democracy," he said. In a way, of course, he was right. But not exactly. Typically, a university is not a democracy in the sense that not everyone gets to vote about what is taught and how (although there are exceptions, I'm told, for example in the Cambridge colleges in the UK)—but more typically, it is a hierarchically organized cooperative society, perhaps better to say a federation, of experts with different competencies, who share responsibility for its critical social mission. Trustees usually have the final say and administrators recommend action about faculty and students to them. But a certain division of labor is also the norm. Ideally, each group should respect the others' competencies in their processes of decision-making. Of course, the dangers of trustee or administrative overreach are sometimes as troubling as interference from politicians and financial patrons, but so are calls from the Right (we are hearing lots of this in the US these days) for students' right of free speech to determine what is taught, and for "substantive neutrality" or balanced interpretations in the classroom. Post's reply to this movement seems right to me: "Disciplines do not create expert knowledge through a market place of ideas in which content discrimination is prohibited and all ideas are deemed equal."[19] Although

---

[19] Ibid., 17.

there are often conflicts within disciplines about what counts as acceptable work—critical new ideas are not always granted validity and there
have been long struggles by scholars (feminists, poststructuralists, critical
race theorists, queer theorists) to achieve legitimacy for their fields of
study—still it is academic freedom and not student free speech that
informs these struggles.

If academic freedom is the prerogative of a specialized group of professional intellectuals, and if the university in which they work is not
technically a democracy, on what basis can the university claim its rights?
Why is it that academic freedom has been the cry of university presidents
and faculty facing unprecedented attacks by authoritarian politicians in
Turkey, Poland, Hungary and lately, in the United States?

It may be paradoxical to argue that democracy depends on the university even if the university is not itself a perfect democracy. But that is the
case. It is the case because critical thinking—Kant's notion of reason in
the face of power, or Dewey's idea that innovation depended on challenging "deep-rooted prejudice," or Said's insistence that "freedom cannot
simply be reduced to venerating the unexamined authority of a national
identity and its culture"—critical thinking is the life-blood of democratic societies; without it all visions of justice and hope are lost."[20] Critical
thinking depends on informed and disciplined knowledge, on our ability
to search for, and to teach our students *how* to search for truth. That kind
of teaching is not a democratic process; it cannot be one. And yet democracy depends on it. (Real democracy, I should add. "Illiberal democracy" is
an oxymoron.)

When the state finds itself at odds with critical thinking, we know that
the search for truth has been shut down; when populist orators decry the

 [20] Said, "Identity, Authority and Freedom: The Potentate and the Traveler," 223.

elitism of the academic establishment, we know that knowledge production is being directed to nefarious ends; when what Said called the
"secular" dimension of critique (its refusal of transcendent explanations
for human life, whether based on history, god, or nature) is replaced by
invocations of essentialism, the borders of knowledge are being closed
and the search for truth, in whatever realm, is canceled. The denial of academic freedom to its universities, of permission to pursue truth wherever it leads, signals the ultimate failure of democracy. And it does not bode
well for the future prosperity and health of the nation.

Public and Private

One of the ironies of the current relationship between universities and
nations is that the most endangered institutions are the ones once considered the most democratic—the public universities supported by the
state. Those universities which are open to students at minimal tuition
costs, depend on the state for financial support but also, legally, the state
has ultimate authority to determine their future. Indeed, it is often in the
name of protecting the public's financial interest that politicians justify
their intervention in curricular and faculty domains. It is those universities which most easily succumb to the demand that (as Said put it) "intellectual discourse must worship at the altar of national identity,"[21] and so
succumb to the suppression of critical inquiry that is the inevitable result.

The resurgence of strong nationalist tendencies is evident across the
world, at least in part, as a reaction to the rise of globalization and its
undermining of the frontiers of national sovereignty. The reassertion of
the importance of the nation is, arguably, the populist response to the
crisis of neo-liberal capitalism. This has brought with it the test of patriotism for all manner of intellectual work—a patriotism that is antithetical
to free thought and the academic freedom that protects it. In the US, we

---

[21] Ibid., 222.

have the example of the Secretary of Education, Betsy DeVos, warning university students that "the fight against the education establishment extends to you too. The faculty, from adjunct professor to deans, tell you what to do, what to say, and more ominously what to think." For DeVos the job of educators to teach students *how* to think is beside the point. Her notion of freedom of thought is the expression of opinion, unconstrained by the requirements of truth or rigor. The real problem for her, as for those seeking to consolidate their power at all costs, is that critique will expose the abuses that necessarily accompany authoritarian rule.

In the modern period, new private universities have grown alongside public ones, often to represent special interests that weren't being served adequately in the public realm. The numbers of the new private universities vary widely from country to country, as does their relationship to the state. Usually there is some kind of contractual agreement that recognizes their legitimacy as degree-granting institutions, but they tend to have greater independence than their public counterparts. In the US, as elsewhere, many private universities were originally founded by religious groups, but that was not exclusively the case. And even those that were originally religious have become increasingly secular, as is the case with the American universities in Cairo and Beirut or with Boğaziçi University in Istanbul.[22] Some private universities were established to provide a more elite environment for students of the upper classes, or for those with financial means but who were ineligible for admission to public schools. Although private universities typically require state certification, they are less susceptible to direct intervention than are state-supported institutions whose financial interest gives the state greater power to intervene.

---

[22] Boğaziçi is now fully administered by the state, but with a special status in relation to other state universities linked to its private origins.

That is why private institutions have been able to preserve something of the critical spirit in the face of all-out assaults on higher education by those seeking to consolidate nationalist identities and to eliminate not just opposition, but the kind of thinking that would call rulers to account for the violations of principle and justice they undertake. Of course, private universities are subject to pressures from donors and politicians— they are not immune from attempts to rein in critique and to control what is studied. Nor are they free of the neo-liberal processes that are everywhere undermining the substance and ethos of a classical university education. But, still, they occupy a privileged place in the realm of academe and that privilege has made them, in our time, the custodians of academic freedom in the sense I have been talking about it—as the protection of the search for truth wherever it leads, of the spirit of critical inquiry that, at its best, refuses compromise.

If, in the US, the University of Wisconsin is no longer a place that allows for the "continual and fearless sifting and winnowing by which alone the truth can be found," private institutions remain in a better position to promote that legacy. It is on their campuses that it is still possible to teach freely and to resist interference—the call for academic freedom resonates with the values and principles to which they at least nominally aspire.

I think that is the case for CEU here in Hungary. It has long been able to stand apart from the currents and passions of successive political regimes. It has also long been a training ground for the leadership of movements for social justice, the rule of law, and the creation of open societies in the region. On the one hand, one might ask how a small graduate institution could pose a serious threat to a government with vast military and police resources at its disposal. On the other hand, the fact of the attack signals the danger that the quest for truth by critical thinkers is seen to pose to authoritarian rule. The frightening aspect of this is that power is on the side of the state. Indeed, the resolution of the crisis might well come from a negotiation between two sovereign entities—the state of NY and the nation of Hungary!

But there is also a hopeful side to the story. It suggests that despite the lamentations of scholars about the end of the university as we knew it—about what Bill Readings called "the university in ruins"[23] and Chris Newfield deemed "the unmaking"[24] of the university—there is something that persists against great odds. The process of erosion of the academy has been gradual and incomplete, allowing the legacy of Kant and Humboldt to survive, even as its homogenizing cultural function has disappeared. There are pockets of resistance on campuses which honor the principles and practices of truth seeking. We can see this in the calls for academic freedom that echo across the globe, in the thousands of protestors who filled the streets of Budapest, and who also continue to speak out in Turkey, Poland, and the US. We can see it in the international outcry against intellectual repression that refuses to accept defeat. And, perhaps ironically, we can see it, too, in the determination of authoritarian rulers to banish critical thought and the institutions that foster it. Their determination is a measure of the aspirational power of the idea of academic freedom, but it is only aspirational. To get rulers to value and respect it requires a political struggle, the dimensions of which are extremely large.

What is the nature of that political struggle? Does it undermine the pluralism and diversity of views that are the proud values of the search for truth and the production of knowledge? I don't think so. The protection of critical thinking has always involved a confrontation with power. By its very nature it is political. The political struggle I am referring to is not

---

[23] Readings, *The University in Ruins*.
[24] Christopher Newfield, *Unmaking the Public University: The Forty Year Assault on the Middle Class* (Cambridge: Harvard University Press, 2011).

partisan or ideological, rather it commits us to the continued practice of critical thinking; the principle that guides us, that articulates the meaning of our struggle is academic freedom. Critical thinking, in this definition of it, is both the cause and effect of academic freedom.

I leave you, then with a circular argument: we need academic freedom to protect the necessarily non-partisan, but nonetheless political work of critical thinking, even as we must engage in that political/intellectual work to bring academic freedom to life. But the politics of the moment requires more than critical thinking, it requires rallying support for the only guarantee we have that democracy can be saved or restored. I hope this conference will give us the means to think and act on that require-ment: to recognize the importance (to say nothing of the pleasure) of our intellectual work and to find the practical political means to continue to do it. It is the challenge we urgently face, and one we have no choice but to meet.

THE THREAT WITHOUT:
STATE PRACTICES AND BARRIERS TO
ACADEMIC FREEDOM AROUND THE
WORLD

Three Ideas of Academic Freedom ——— *Liviu Matei*

——— *Liviu Matei is Provost and Pro-Rector of Central European University and a Professor of Higher Education Policy at the School of Public Policy.*

In order to design and put in practice policies or other actions that are supportive of academic freedom, it is imperative to understand the relationship between academic freedom and the state. I cannot address this matter here in its entirety but I would like to put forward three ideas that shed light on this relationship, which is "traversed by tensions that are necessary and unresolvable," to use a phrase from Joan Scott's chapter.

The Distinction Between Academic Freedom and University Autonomy

When we try to understand the relationship between academic freedom and the state, it is helpful to make use of the distinction between academic freedom and university autonomy (or institutional autonomy). This distinction is a contested one. Still, it is helpful. Traditionally, academic freedom is understood as the freedom of individual academics and students to teach, study and pursue knowledge and research without unreasonable interference or restriction from law, institutional regulations or public pressure. This resonates with Einstein's often-quoted definition:

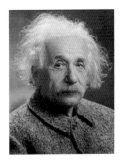

By academic freedom I understand the right to search for truth and to publish and teach what one holds to be true.

University autonomy, on the other hand, is of the institution, not the individual. It is about the right of the university to determine its organization and administrative structures, to decide on priorities, manage its budget, hire personnel and admit students, decide on the content and form of its teaching and research. Very often, when we talk about infringement on academic freedom as interference by the state, we are in reality referring to the restriction of institutional autonomy and not of academic freedom. Academic freedom and institutional autonomy are related, but different. We may say, in fact, that institutional autonomy is a precondition for academic freedom.

To illustrate this, let us take the case of CEU. We can clearly interpret the recent attacks against CEU in Hungary as being directed against university autonomy. The attack of the Hungarian government was not directly against our faculty members or students, against their freedom to pursue the study of a particular subject or publish a paper on a given topic. This was not about censorship of academic work. Rather, it was an attack against our University as an institution, about the right of this institution to decide on how to organize its work, its administrative operations and governance structures.

Matters of academic freedom are more salient in certain countries; in others, it is rather institutional autonomy that is more critical. In the US and Western Europe, institutional autonomy is often taken for granted and what is more debated is academic freedom. In other countries, as in many parts of the post-Soviet region, institutional autonomy is severely restricted, which makes it a more urgent matter to discuss and attend to.

Let me mention Myanmar as an example. This country is an emerging democracy where CEU's Elkana Center for Higher Education has been working intensely for the last five years. There is still almost no institutional autonomy in the country after decades of repressive political regimes, which makes the matter of academic freedom basically irrelevant. All rectors, academics and many administrators are rotated; they are moved from one university to another around the country. The individuals and institutions concerned have no say on who is going where and when. There is no staffing autonomy. Curricula are decided centrally for all disciplines by the Ministry. Universities have no ownership over their buildings, cannot decide on student enrollments or finances. As a consequence, because there is almost no institutional autonomy, the organization of the universities is completely ineffective and there is no genuine research and teaching in the country—there is nothing to be censured, really, as there is no possibility of choosing. For this reason, as the higher education system of the country is beginning to reform, there is no discussion about academic freedom (although academic freedom is nominally recognized by law). The big discussion in Myanmar higher education nowadays is about autonomy as a precondition for genuine university work. It is the state that makes the work of universities impossible, having deprived them of autonomy over many decades. It is also the state that is trying to change this situation, and for the better. CEU has been working in Myanmar with national authorities and the two flagship universities since 2012 to reform system-level regulations and make autonomy possible.

CEU PhD graduate Natalia Peral teaching students during her CEU Global Teaching Fellowship at Mandalay University, Myanmar

Academic Freedom and Institutional Autonomy are Multidimensional

Academic freedom and institutional autonomy are not binary, yes-or-no variables. They are not unidimensional either. Both are multidimensional and are a matter of degree. There is no absolute freedom anywhere. And, importantly, there is at least some freedom in any university at any time. By this, I do not mean to ignore or excuse the reality of severe restrictions and repression of academic freedom and university autonomy in certain countries, going all the way from censorship to imprisonment and even killings of academics and students. Still, speaking of academic freedom, it is important to recognize that in different systems and institutions academics have more freedom or less freedom, as opposed to no freedom at all or complete freedom. They can be free in certain areas but not in others. On the other side, speaking of institutional autonomy, universities in particular national systems may have the right to decide on their own in certain areas but not in others. They can have more freedom in one area and very limited freedom in another. We cannot speak of autonomy as one discreet variable that can be reflected in a single index or measure, but rather as a combination or configuration of dimensions and degrees. This combination should be taken into account to understand properly the university autonomy as a concept and also as a defined condition of a given university or higher education system at a particular time. This blend is fundamentally a result of policies for which the state is ultimately responsible, although other actors might be involved as well. The exact nature of the mix of degrees and dimensions is obviously not without consequences for the work of the university.

Take China for example. Chinese universities have large financial and significant academic autonomy. However, this is not the full picture. What they lack, according to scholars of Chinese higher education,[1] is the right to decide on their long-term priorities and strategic orientation. They lack the so-called "strategic autonomy." While universities can decide by themselves in particular areas, the overall institutional direction is decided by state authorities from the outside. It is, in a way, as if Chinese universities were given by the government powerful cars to drive and a lot of money to buy gas, but they are also given a map by the same government with one single highway they can use, and are not allowed to explore other avenues than what is on the map. And after a while they get another map, with another road. This approach to university autonomy helps to understand the often studied (and deplored) lack of creativity in China (or "why China can't innovate," as formulated by Abrami, Kirby, and McFarlan[2]). It also helps explain that although China has overtaken the US in terms of numbers of academic publications, it lags behind in producing genuine new knowledge that shows creativity.

---

[1] See for example: Qiang Zha and Ruth Hayhoe, "The 'Beijing Consensus' and the Chinese Model of University Autonomy" 9, no. 1 (2014): 42–62.
[2] Regina. M. Abrami, William C. Kirby, and F. Warren McFarlan, "Why China Can't Innovate," *Harvard Business Review*, no. March 2014 (2014).

If academic freedom and institutional autonomy are not binary variables, not yes or no, does this also mean that they cannot be fully repressed? This is an interesting question. Let us take the case of Russia, a hot spot on the global map in the fight for academic freedom and autonomy. In her research, Liza Potapova, a doctoral student and Elkana fellow at CEU, notes that the Russian state in our times has different approaches to different types of freedom. Academic freedom is tolerated, within limits that are at times quite broad, while freedom of association and freedom of speech are severely restricted, to the point on annihilation. Why does the government tolerate, in fact even encourage, academic freedom, albeit within certain limits? The answer in this case is that the Russian government expects something ("returns") from universities: to produce knowledge that is good for economic development, for social mobility and for symbolic reasons (international prestige for the country). The Russian government has the ambition to place five universities in the first 100 of the world by 2020 (the Russian "academic excellence project," also known as "5-100"). It is understood—and accepted—that universities can-not deliver all the state expects from them without autonomy. Therefore, Russian universities and academics are allowed to exercise freedom with-in certain limits. As soon as they confront or challenge the government, or are perceived as such, they overstep the limits and will be repressed. The political factor, the will of the state or powerful politicians, remain important and may play both ways, in support of autonomy or against it. We have seen a "differentiated treatment" of universities in a single city, St. Petersburg. Colleagues at the Higher School of Economics, whose university is flourishing, publish wonderful research and have a robust educational program. They have been careful not only to build a strong academic basis for the institution, but also to avoid going on a collision course with the government. At the same time, the more independent European University, another good academic institution in the same city, is facing the risk of being closed down. More than just "differentiated," this case illustrates a somewhat discretionary treatment of universities, academic freedom and autonomy, which might be common characteristic of illiberal regimes. Still, academic freedom does exist in Russia, as it exists in other regimes that can be considered authoritarian.

Another example is the higher education miracle of Singapore. Good universities have been created top-down in Singapore with a lot of financial support from the government but with little, almost no institutional autonomy at the beginning in some key areas. That has changed because the government expected to achieve certain broader objectives (universities to fulfill precise "goals" defined by the government) and these universities could not deliver without autonomy. Now, basically all great Singaporean universities describe themselves as autonomous.

These examples speak to the degree to which the state can tolerate, even encourage and support academic freedom and institutional autonomy in non-democratic regimes.

We can also go back to the question whether academic freedom can be completely suppressed. We can discuss for a moment the example of science in Soviet universities during the Stalin era. There was a lot of excellent scientific production on the backdrop of complete absence of democracy. Did academics produce outstanding research only in disciplines that were programmatically encouraged by the government for specific political reasons (arms race, for example) or also in disciplines that it simply neglected? Did they produce good research because in reality they had some degree of academic freedom, even in a severely authoritarian regime? Is this something we can conceptualize simply in terms of "freedom of thinking"? These are some of the key questions we need to ask in order to understand the relationship between academic freedom, university autonomy, and the state.

Universities Need the State

Universities need a state around them. They cannot operate well without state institutions and regulations to protect them and make their work possible, including by creating the conditions for academic freedom and institutional autonomy. The state is always an important actor, even in countries with a strong tradition of self-regulation. The state remains crucially important even as international education expands continuously and dramatically. The state is not disappearing from higher education in the age of internationalization.

Perhaps surprisingly, CEU itself is a good illustration for the continuing key role of the state. We are an international university, possibly one of the most international in the world. That is not only because we hire faculty and enroll students from almost all countries of the world, but also because we are one of the very few universities worldwide without a national majority in the student body. Also, we do not have a national intellectual agenda or curriculum. Still, we recently clashed with a particular state, the Hungarian state, to the point that our very existence was at stake, at least here in Hungary. To address this, we sought the support of various non-state national and international constituencies and this support did come in, overwhelmingly. But it still might not work, as it did not work in the case of universities in Turkey, where international support changed nothing because the government did not change its stand. It looks like our best chance is another state, the State of New York, which is now negotiating with Hungary so that the Hungarian government puts in place regulations and legislation that protect rather that undermine our institutional integrity, and allows us to continue. We are an international university, and yet we absolutely need the support of a state, to guarantee our autonomy and, to a large degree, our academic freedom as well. We cannot work otherwise. We are an international university, but we cannot be stateless, we cannot operate without a state around us.

Lessons from CEU and Other Universities

What we learn from this short analysis, I believe, is something that might not be comfortable and easy to accept. It is a reaffirmation of the old Humboldtian principle that it is the responsibility of the state to protect the university, to ensure its autonomy and also the conditions for its academic freedom. And there is something more frightening here—and if I am proven wrong I would be happy to accept it. Only the state can ensure autonomy, not civil society, or other non-state actors, including international actors. Look at the demonstrations in Hungary. As impressive and large as they were, they did not change much by themselves. Nor can international organizations fulfill this role—just see the minimal effects of the Council of Europe or the European Union putting pressure on Turkey and Hungary. The same applies to the broader "international community" or the "court or the public opinion." Here again, if we look at Turkey currently, or consider the situation in higher education in Serbia under Milosevic, international pressure could not change the state of affairs with regard to autonomy. The Serbian Parliament adopted a repressive new law on higher education in 1998, with immediate and drastic effects on autonomy, affecting the work of all universities, many academics, students, and administrators. The adoption and brutal implementation of the law generated a broad and strong reaction in Europe by many universities and organizations working in higher education, which advocated restoring the academic and managerial autonomy of Serbian universities. Only that the law stayed in place until the regime changed altogether. These examples do not mean that civil society, international organizations or universities themselves don't have a role and responsibility. But the key, I would say, is in the hand of the state. The state can turn academic freedom on and off. Non-state actors must engage directly with the state to have an impact.

This is the second important lesson here. In order to have good arrangements for university autonomy as a pre-condition for academic freedom, we need to engage with the state. This might sound trivial, but it is not at all. Think of the international organizations, foundations that are doing capacity-building in countries where there is no or limited institutional autonomy, and do this by working exclusively with universities in those countries. This approach is wrong. Those who want to help, from the outside, must engage directly with the state as well. One cannot ensure autonomy working only with or on universities. Remember that the key is in the hand of the state.

A final question: if we accept that we need to engage with the state, can this work—and if yes, how? When I say "we," I mean whether we are a particular university directly engaged in acquiring, defending or promoting its own autonomy or other actors (other universities, international organizations, etc.) trying to help. This is a long discussion. I would only like to say, based on direct experience, that engagement with the state can work. Let me give one example. The CEU Elkana Center has done a lot of work in Myanmar over the past few years trying to support capacity-building in universities but also to promote changing the national regulatory framework with regard to autonomy. Last summer we were invited by the new Minister of Education in the fabulous city of Naypyidaw. He started the meeting by quoting the eight dimensions of university autonomy we proposed in the Practical Handbook on University Autonomy that we prepared two years earlier to inform the discussions regarding the reform in this area in Myanmar.[3] We have done this work in direct and stubborn contact with national authorities, starting already with the last military government, and it looks like this approach worked. We also learned in the meeting with the Minister that the drafting committee for the new higher education law (still to be adopted at this time) has put language

[3] Liviu Matei and Julia Iwinska, "University Autonomy: a Practical Handbook" (Budapest, 2014).

from our Handbook into the draft higher education law. It is remarkable and unexpected that a small university like CEU may have an impact in a large country 7,000 miles away, but this example does show that engagement with the state and national authorities for the cause of promoting institutional autonomy is possible and can be effective.

Academic Freedom in the UK, the Indian Subcontinent and Bangladesh —— *Nirmala Rao*

—— *Nirmala Rao is Vice Chancellor of the Asian University for Women, Chittagong, Bangladesh*

I would like to offer some reflections based on my experience of working and studying in the UK and in India. Earlier in January this year, I took up the position of Vice Chancellor of the Asian University for Women (AUW) based in Chittagong, Bangladesh. Established in 2008, AUW is neither a private nor a public university; rather an international university funded predominantly by individual donors, corporations, trusts and foundations. It enjoys considerable academic freedom, with the Board of Trustees drawn from all over the world. The Board is chaired by the former Foreign Minister of Bangladesh and has two ex-official members as trustees, including the Secretary for Education and the Secretary for Foreign Affairs. Nearly 60% of our faculty are from overseas, primarily from North America. So, unlike other public and private universities in Bangladesh, AUW enjoys immense academic autonomy by virtue of its international status. However, in the wider context, academic freedom in both India and Bangladesh is increasingly under threat and the crisis includes academics being subject to severe sanctions including suspension, firing, imprisonment and even violence.

Academic Freedom in the UK

In the UK, such freedom, though real, is relatively intangible, compared with other countries, due primarily to the absence of any formal guarantees of liberty in the British Constitution. Despite this, academic freedom has always been taken for granted and freedom of thought and speech is among the most prized civil liberties in the UK. But recently there have been growing political and social pressures which have become a serious menace to academic freedom in British universities. In the past, religious pressures were more problematic: they were an outstanding feature of the middle years of the 19th century at Oxford and Cambridge and mainly responsible for setting up University College London (UCL) and King's College in 1828 and 1832 respectively and, indeed, the University of Durham in 1832. By comparison, in most European countries, as we all know, Universities have always been state institutions, and professors and teachers predominantly either civil servants or in the last resort subjected to state control. However, those who created the new universities of the 20th century in the UK took the contrary view that universities should be self-governing, autonomous institutions.[1]

Pressures in the English context are changing, including the rapidly increasing financial dominance of central government, pressures of growing expenditure and pressures from regulatory bodies. More importantly, proponents of business interests fund research projects in universities, who cannot reasonably be expected to provide funds unconditionally and without accountabilities. That said, it is difficult to judge how far this indeterminable pressures on the scientific and technological departments of British universities has become a menace to academic freedom over time.

The changing nature of funding for UK research increasingly determines the nature of dissemination of research findings into the public domain.

[1] Lord Chorley, "Academic Freedom in the United Kingdom," *Law and Contemporary Problems* 28, no. 3 (January 1963): 647, http://www.jstor.org/stable/1190651?origin=crossref.

This includes the dominance of the research excellence framework, the economistic approach of the research councils and the commercialization of research that dictate priorities. Likewise, the Teaching Excellence Framework determines the level of fees universities can charge, which in turn depends on how well institutions perform on a range of quality measures. As I speak the results of the Teaching Excellence Framework were released this morning.

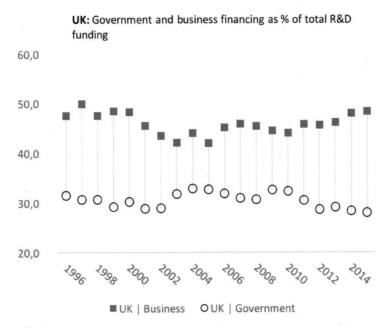

UK: Government and business financing as % of total R&D funding

Figure 1. Source: UNESCO, Global gross expenditure on research and development

The question we must answer is how far the existing arrangements within universities ensure academic freedom? When terms and appointments, conditions of appointment and dismissal of staff remain in the hands of authorities, they can seriously curtail freedom. The freedom of an individual teacher to write, teach and research according to his or her consciousness depends in the last resort on him being safeguarded from dismissal, should one's attitude and actions become displeasing to the university authorities. Academic freedom depends much more on tradition, on the culture of the organization and driven by public perceptions rather than by legally established rules.

British universities also seem more intent on monitoring and controlling the way in which academic staff take part in public debates. The University of Leeds attracted media attention a couple of years ago for using its social media policies to reprimand a lecturer who publicly criticized the Home Secretary. Under the name of counter-terrorism, further regulations were conceived. There is a growing climate of self-censorship on campus as well as a sense that some issues, particularly related to security and anti-terrorism, are too 'hot' to handle. More recently we've seen demands from students for greater racial sensitivity and representation of non-white cultures at the institutions. Campaigns by students in universities such as Oxford and the School of Oriental and African Studies have called for the de-colonization of the curriculum and the campus. At Oxford, protesters removed the statues of colonial figures like Rhodes or Christopher Codrington, while at SOAS protesters removed white philosophers to bring the curriculum and reading list in line with the School's focus on Asia, Africa and the Middle East.[2] They argued that they are too Euro-centric and ignore works by people of color.

Academic Freedom and the Indian Subcontinent

Academic freedom is at the crossroads at the Indian subcontinent. The role of universities and the ability of academic staff to speak out on

---

[2] Aftab Ali, "Oxford University Students Call for Greater 'Racial Sensitivity' at the Institution and Say It Must Be 'Decolonised' | The Independent," *Independent*, 2015, http://www.independent.co.uk/student/news/oxford-university-students-call-for-greater-racial-sensitivity-at-the-institution-and-say-it-must-be-10332118.html.

a range of issues has become a central concern. Power and control have become more centralized, resulting in a dramatic decrease of faculty autonomy. Instead of providing oversight and overall coordination, administrators are taking decisions, even academic decisions, with less input from faculty. Faculty who openly disagree with administration can be reprimanded, actions that are generally supported by courts. One by-product of this is the appointment of people for academic positions who support government policies. And we've been seeing a lot more of this since 2014, when the current ruling party appointed senior administrators who support the political party and also support student-led groups, which align themselves with the ruling party. They can silence any opposition on campus, those who are not in line with the current government's policies and those from the opposition who do not necessarily agree with the policies of the day. Although free press and democratic elections are the norm, free speech is circumscribed to conform to cultural and religious norms. Documentaries and films exploring religious conflicts have been withdrawn on many campuses after individuals received threats. Controversial issues conflicting with society, such as caste and gender-related issues, frequently create a climate that manifests itself in a lack of support or validation for research. The result is that academics develop a sense of what can be researched and what is better left unstudied and unquestioned.

Let me put forward a couple of examples. The award-winning book on the Hindus by the former President of the American Academy of Religions, Wendy Doniger, is banned from Indian classrooms because traditionalists view the text as an attack on Hinduism. Another book by Doniger on Hinduism was also placed under review by experts before reprinting.[3] This practice of either banning a book or forcing a severe backlash is becoming increasingly

[3] William Tierney and Nidhi S. Sabharwal, "Debating Academic Freedom in India," *AAUP Journal of Academic Freedom* 7 (2016), https://www.aaup.org/JAF7/debating-academic-freedom-india#.WbD-bMhJZTM.

common. What one writes and studies can result in suspension of services, public controversy, withholding or suspension of publications. I know this sounds very dramatic but that is the reality in India now. Two universities prohibited professors from addressing the media after academics made statements criticizing anti-terrorism policies. The Nobel Prize winner Amartya Sen stepped down as Vice Chancellor of the newly created Nalanda University because of what he perceived as governmental attacks on academic freedom.[4] 'Scholars at Risk,' the human rights organization devoted to the protection of academic freedom, has published numerous accounts of Indian academics who have been arrested, beaten or in some instances imprisoned or killed, because of what they've said in the classroom or what they've written. There is a real fear both in India and Bangladesh of vigilante reaction for unpopular or uncommon ideas in both countries.

India: Number of incidents reported by Scholars at risk infringing academic freedom and/or the human rights of members of higher education communities

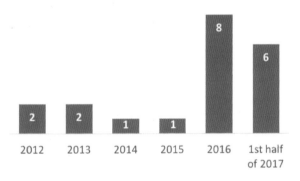

Figure 2. Source: Scholars at Risk: Academic Freedom Monitor

[4] Amartya Sen, "Academic Freedom Becoming Alien Thought in India: Amartya Sen - Times of India," *The Times of India*, February 22, 2017, http://timesofindia.indiatimes. com/business/india-business/academic-freedom-becoming-alien-thought-in-india-amartya-sen/articleshow/57291168.cms.

Bangladesh: Number of incidents reported by Scholars at risk infringing academic freedom and/or the human rights of members of higher education communities

| 2013 | 2014 | 2015 | 2016 |

Figure 3. Source: Scholars at Risk: Academic Freedom Monitor

Curricula in India and in Bangladesh are another issue. They are centrally prescribed. Committees create courses, syllabi with readings, and professors are instructed to teach from those materials. If one wants to deviate from the curriculum, permission needs to be granted by the faculty committee and ultimately governmental authority. The result is that an instructor who wishes to teach for example, Salman Rushdie's *Satanic Verses* or the recently banned *India's Daughter*, a 2015 documentary by Leslee Udwin about the rape that occurred in New Delhi, would be unable to use either.[5]

In cases like this, autonomy is curtailed and academic freedom infringed.

All these examples speak of the governmental intrusion into the affairs of the university and the limits of academic freedom. In some worst cases individuals are harassed, jailed or physically harmed. Academic freedom to teach and conduct research without fear becomes even more important in a system undergoing massification such as in India, where the social composition of students in universities has moved from being elite homogeneous to a much more diverse body. That diversity in itself

---

[5] Tierney and Sabharwal, "Debating Academic Freedom in India."

brings students with different backgrounds and different ideologies, who have a very different view of understanding and shaping what academic freedom is all about.

I want to conclude by saying that my own inclination is to ask, how do these developments alter the state's responsibility to protect incursions into academic freedom? Can an increasingly intolerant society accommodate academic freedom at all? And what do formal liberties mean, if destructive intangibles can so easily erode protections otherwise provided? With those questions in mind, my own pessimistic bias is to say that academic freedom cannot operate in the medieval mode of gated communities. Intolerance outside will gulf every community and the university will be no exception. Academic freedom and tolerance need to be cultivated as public and civic virtues. Without these, these values will become even more vulnerable, so that the shield of the university cannot protect them anymore from the waiting assaults.

Academic Freedom and Universities in Continental Europe —— *Helga Nowotny*

—— Helga Nowotny is the former President of the European Research Council (2010-2013). She is Professor Emerita of Social Studies of Science, ETH Zurich.

Several commentators in this volume, for example Allison Stanger, raise the question about the fragility of our values. We have seen a rise of populism and nationalism almost everywhere in Europe even if, for the moment, we are in a period of respite and hope. But we do not know how long it will last and it raises a terrifying question for all of us to answer: Can democracies die?

I will focus on the universities I know best, the universities in continental Europe. The focus is often on the Anglo-Saxon model as described by Nirmala Rao. But the continental model is, despite considerable variation, more widespread. The continental model is based on public universities. It is largely state-funded universities, although private universities exist too. For the most part, these universities don't have campuses and campus life nor campus governance and everything that goes with it. Yet there are structural similarities which all universities have in common. Relating to Jonathan Cole's commentary, I would also argue that what makes a good university, no matter where it is or how it is governed, is the fact that it must be upsetting. Therefore, I want to explore the question: What is upsetting nowadays in continental European universities?

I would like to start with some historical contextualization. There were two historical watersheds in the recent period of continental European universities. The first one was the end of communism. Hungary as well as other former communist countries have been struggling with reconstructing and modernizing their universities. The second break came with the developments that occurred in Western Europe around 1968. This was the time of student revolts, and the experience was very upsetting. It brought the end of a long historical period of the German type of *Ordinarienuniversität*, the hierarchical university. The student revolt broke the monopoly of this type of university. It occurred among other changes within the wider society. In France, Servan-Schreiber lamented in the late 1960s about Europe being left behind compared to the US in terms

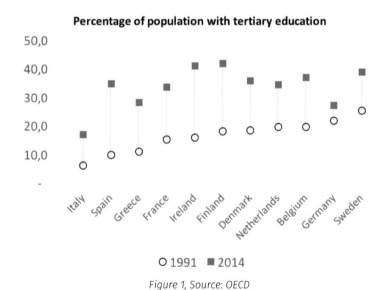

Percentage of population with tertiary education

O 1991 ■ 2014

Figure 1, Source: OECD

of innovation and economic competitiveness. In the US, Harvey Brooks, an astute science-policy adviser who was also advising the OECD, wrote an influential report urging European political leaders to open up their universities for a higher percentage of their citizens to enroll in higher education as a necessary step to boost economic competitiveness.

What were the effects of these developments? With the opening of the universities, student numbers increased. The opening was accompanied by waves of so-called democratizations within universities and governance structures were changed. Professors now had to share their decisionmaking

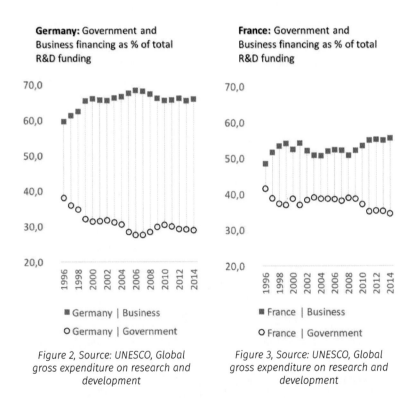

Germany: Government and Business financing as % of total R&D funding

■ Germany | Business
○ Germany | Government

Figure 2, Source: UNESCO, Global gross expenditure on research and development

France: Government and Business financing as % of total R&D funding

■ France | Business
○ France | Government

Figure 3, Source: UNESCO, Global gross expenditure on research and development

power with students, with representatives of the administration and with younger colleagues. This resulted partly in chaotic situations that could not last. Besides, being state-funded meant that some hidden interdependency with the state and ministries that were providing the funding were maintained. The road towards university autonomy was and still is a long one.

It also became clear that the aspired democratization was not compatible with the ideal of efficiency as preached by neoliberalism. Starting in the UK and increasingly brought to continental Europe, universities introduced audits, assessments and evaluations of all kinds. Universities are held accountable and have to sign complex performance agreements, detailing their teaching, research and outreach obligations. All of this is now taken for granted. It has become part of university governance. The downside is that for many continental European universities, the broad mission of taking in increasing student numbers was not matched by adequate increases in state funding. There was increasing pressure inside universities to cope with limited resources. There is now outside pressure to perform according to numerous assessment and benchmarking exercises. If one looks at international university rankings, continental European universities tend to have a very bad student-staff ratio which pushes them down in the overall rankings.

So, these are some of the upsetting pressures that European universities are exposed to right now. What is most upsetting, however, is the loss of free time. Time has become an extremely scarce resource. It comes with the loss of experimental spaces inside the university, spaces for discussion and generating new ideas. The Humboldtian ideal, referred to by several contributors in this publication, seems to be on its way out. But you don't have to go back to Humboldt's time. Most members of my generation have experienced their student life as something where we enjoyed lots of time and freedom to discuss, engaging in topics related to our naive beliefs

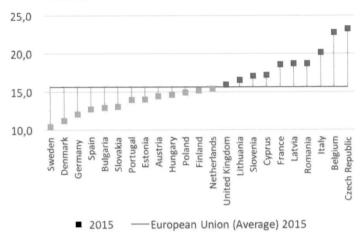

Ratio of students to academic staff in tertiary education in the EU

■ 2015 ——European Union (Average) 2015

Figure 4, Source: Eurostat

of how to improve the world—all this is threatened to be lost. This is the greatest threat that I see for most continental European universities now.

What is to be done? I think we have to engage much more with what is happening at the interface, the multiple exchanges and various kinds of communications that take place between science and society. I see a difference here between Europe and the US. The difference is partly rooted in the 19th century concept of Wissenschaft which still pervades Scandinavian languages, Dutch, German and others. Wissenschaft is inclusive and the social sciences and humanities are part of it. In Anglo-Saxon countries, science means the natural sciences only, excluding the social sciences and humanities. This is a fundamentally different way of looking at the world. This idea of science being one, the concept of Wissenschaft, makes it easier to reach out and communicate with society. It enables to bring what happens in society into the university and universities may respond by becoming 'unsettling'.

Altering the relationship between science and society started with the natural sciences. They were first in line when a loss of trust set in, beginning with the nuclear power controversy, followed by controversies about genetically modified organisms and others. Those were big topics discussed inside and outside the university. Natural scientists had to respond to the challenge. At first, they reacted rather naively, thinking it is enough to inform the public. They had to learn quickly that this simply does not work. What followed were various bottom-up initiatives, partly helped through state-sponsored initiatives to stimulate more public engagement on the part of university researchers. Thus, the idea of citizen science emerged and these various efforts created a window of opportunity to speak with society and to listen to what society has to say. Paradoxically, the social sciences were late in this engagement. The pressure was less and many social scientists thought that they are in contact with society anyhow, knowing what's going on. However, there is a key difference in doing research on people and doing research with people.

I'm not trying to paint an ideal picture here of European continental universities. They are far from being a mirror of society, although the ideal of meritocracy implies to include the most talented from wherever they come. We have done rather badly in terms of diversity if one looks, for instance, at student numbers from the generation with a migration background. Universities have not kept up with the way ethnic diversity has become part of European societies today. There is a lot of work to be done also in trying to anticipate what kind of solutions European societies will need for the problems of tomorrow. In order to be 'unsettling,' universities need to be competent, but also to have the courage to live up to their ideals. This is what CEU has done and hopefully will be able to continue doing.

Academic Freedom: The Global Challenge and the Case of Turkey —— Ayşe Kadıoğlu

—— Ayşe Kadıoğlu is Professor of Political Science at Sabancı University, Istanbul.

It is a pleasure to be here at CEU, a university that is resisting closure in an exemplary way. Indeed, you empower us all. I am here as a member of a university in Turkey whose faculty members have engaged in a number of joint academic research projects with faculty members at CEU. I am also here as a member of the academy in a country where academic freedoms eroded in an unprecedented magnitude during the past year. There was a bloody coup d'état attempt in July 2016 that resulted in the death of 250 citizens, most of whom were people who went out to the streets to stop the coup. Since the failed coup attempt, over 5,000 academics in public and private universities have lost their jobs.

1,128 academics calling themselves "Academics for Peace" signed a statement in January 2016 calling for a peaceful resolution of the conflict and an end to the ongoing atrocities against Kurdish citizens in the southeastern provinces of Turkey and saying: "we won't be a party to this crime." This is what you would normally expect from public intellectuals in the face of human suffering and that is exactly what they were doing with this statement. Yet, this act resulted in the imprisonment and purge of many of these academics who signed the statement.

In the aftermath of the state of emergency, academics have been facing a series of purges. The biggest purge came on September 1, 2016, when 40,000 public employees were dismissed, including 2,346 academics who were purged from various universities in Turkey. Another big purge came on October 29, 2016, resulting in the dismissal of 1,267 academics, followed by the purge of 631 academics on January 6, 2017; and 335 academics on February 7, 2017. The most recent purge prior to this conference at CEU came on April 29, 2017 when 484 academics from various universities were purged (the figures were gathered from the website of Scholars at Risk).

All of these purges were realized though executive decrees that are –as we all know- prevalent measures in states of emergency. After the July coup d'état attempt, 15 universities with alleged links to the religious community led by Fethullah Gülen, viewed as the main culprit behind the coup d'état attempt, were closed. Many colleagues were imprisoned. Some are unable to leave the country because their passports were confiscated. There have been two cases of suicide. My dear colleague Umut Özkirimli published an article in the latest issue of the journal *Globalizations* titled: "How to Liquidate a People" which is a tribute to one of these academics.[1] There has also been a hunger strike by an academic and a teacher. They were arrested on the 76th day of their strike. The hunger strike continues and in terms of permanent damage to their health, they have passed the point of no return.

Some academics left the country either by resigning from their positions and finding employment abroad or through sabbaticals and unpaid leaves. Some are unable to leave since their passports have been re-

---

[1] Umut Özkirimli, "How to Liquidate a People? Academic Freedom in Turkey and Beyond," *Globalizations*, May 22, 2017, 1–6, doi:10.1080/14747731.2017.1325171.

voked. Some are persistent in staying. It is not easy to stay, but it is not easy to leave either. Scholars in Turkey are finding themselves more and more cornered while still feeling a sense of responsibility towards their undergraduate and graduate students who continue their studies. The predominant feeling among them is one of frustration and desperation.

It is not the first time in the history of the Turkish Republic that members of the academic community are facing challenges. There were similar moments in 1933, 1948 or after the 1960 and the 1980 military coups. The 1933 purge was followed by the employment of Jewish professors who were deported from Nazi Germany although their European identity was more emphasized than their Jewish identity at the time since that would be in line with the Turkish state's official rhetoric of Westernization. The main motive behind the 1948 purge was anti-communism, leading to a communist witch hunt in universities. These were followed by purges in the aftermath of the 1960 and 1980 military coups. Still, the academic purges of the past year are quite different in terms of scope, intensity and magnitude. There is an atmosphere of paralysis since many purged academics are unable to leave the country and accept employment offers in other countries for their passports have been confiscated. Many academics argue that those who are purged are virtually sentenced to a "civilian death" without trial since they cannot take public office anywhere else and are not hired by private institutions for fear of retribution.

There is an emphasis laid on the global challenge to academic freedoms in this conference. I think, what I have just described points to the extraordinary state of the academy in Turkey. Nevertheless, I believe the global challenge is also there albeit in a different magnitude.

When President Trump signed an executive order at the end of January blocking entry to the US by the citizens of Iran, Iraq, Libya, Somalia, Sudan, Syria, and Yemen; 17 prestigious universities including Harvard, Yale, and Stanford launched a legal challenge to this ban. They underlined that the ban threatened their ability to attract international students and academics they needed to meet their goals of "educating tomorrow's leaders from around the world." In a joint statement, the universities declared that "by prohibiting persons from freely traveling to and from this country, the executive order divides students and their families, impairs the ability of American universities to draw the finest international talent, and inhibits the free exchange of ideas."[2]

The president of Johns Hopkins University—which is among the 17 universities legally challenging the ba—said that the executive order "takes our country down the ominous path of erecting barriers not on the basis of a demonstrated security threat but on the basis of religion." He also said that "the order stands in unambiguous opposition to our country's long-cherished values and ideals."[3]

On February 10, 2017, the Deans of Yale and Harvard Law Schools, Robert Post and Martha Minow, respectively, published an op-ed in the Boston Globe titled "Standing Up for 'So-called' Law."[4] The title of the piece was in response to a tweet by Donald Trump, who mocked and referred to Judge James Robart who blocked the travel ban as a "so-called judge." President Trump tweeted: "The opinion of this so-called judge, which essentially takes law enforcement away from our country, is ridiculous and will be overturned!" The op-ed by the deans of Yale and Harvard Law Schools is of historical importance. They state the following:

[2] Harriet Agerholm, "Harvard, Yale and Stanford Sue Donald Trump over His 'Muslim Travel Ban,'" The Independent, February 14, 2017, http://www.independent.co.uk/news/world/americas/harvard-yale-stanford-suing-donald-trump-muslim-ban-law-suit-us-immigration-restriction-a7579886.html.
[3] Ibid.
[4] Martha Minow and Robert Post, "Standing up for 'so-Called' Law," *Boston Globe*, February 10, 2017, https://www.bostonglobe.com/opinion/2017/02/10/standing-for-called-law/VLbDYmrwpdjCn8qs5FPJaK/story.html.

We are deans of respected law schools. We have dedicated our professional lives to the proposition that law over- rides violence with reason. Law stands for what we have in common, not merely what divides us. Law respects dis- agreement; it patiently considers evidence and advocacy; it engages with the views of all. Each person—not just each citizen—is equal before the law (...) If Trump believes he can make an enemy of the law and of the Constitution, then he has truly become a foe of the Republic, despite the oath he swore at his inauguration. The craft and professional culture of law is what makes politics possible; it is what keeps poli- tics from spiraling into endless violence. By questioning the legitimacy and authority of judges, Trump seems perilously close to characterizing the law as simply one more enemy to be smashed into submission. At risk are the legal practices and protections that guard our freedom and our safety from the mob violence that destroyed democracies in the 1930s (...) If we are to keep the rule of law, it must not be a parti- san question; it must not be the concern simply of lawyers. We must all defend it, passionately and whole-heartedly. Without the rule of law, we may have a "so-called" presi- dent who has in fact become a tyrant. Fundamentally, this moment is not about Trump. It is about all of us.[5]

These are historically significant statements of our times. They empower all academics around the globe who are staging a fight not only to main- tain academic freedom but also freedom of expression, two significantly distinct phenomena.

When we talk about setting a high standard for free speech, we almost always mean the freedom of speech of those with whom we disagree or

[5] Ibid.

who have ideas we may even find distasteful. I think that one must fight hateful speech not by repression but by more speech. Hateful speech cannot be effectively condemned by means of "hiding behind the robes of judges" but rather uplifting public deliberation (an expression used by Timothy Garton Ash in 2011).[6] In the US, this is called the First Amendment tradition. How, then, is it possible to uphold such a standard under the existing conditions in Turkey? What can you do as a scholar when you encounter executive decrees that lead to the purge of thousands of academics, the closure of universities, and travel bans? What do you do when your ideals and the reality on the ground are oceans apart? How can you be a scholar upholding ideas akin to the First Amendment tradition in a place where academics are imprisoned for speaking their minds and putting their signature on a statement against violence and for peace? How can you continue to be a scholar when nuances are lost; when a topography of concrete prevails?

To conclude, I would like to emphasize a point Joan Scott made about the tension between raison and raison d'état, between truth and state power. When a state with all its authorities regards itself under siege, due process and reason are inevitably lost. Living in an environment where reason is surrendered to raison d'état is like the death of intellect and wisdom. It signals the "triumph of the will" (as in the film by Leni Riefenstahl commissioned by the Nazis). In my first book (1999, in Turkish) titled, *Cumhuriyet Iradesi, Demokrasi Muhakemesi* (Republican will, democratic reason), I had underlined how upholding the will to follow in primary and secondary school education can be detrimental for democratic ideals.[7] Whenever the will to follow a pre-designed path is glorified over reason, intellectual conflict is eliminated and one is encouraged to take sides in

[6] Timothy Garton Ash, "To Fight the Xenophobic Populists, We Need More Free Speech, Not Less," *The Guardian*, May 12, 2011, https://www.theguardian.com/commentisfree/2011/may/12/fight-xenophobic-populists-need-free-speech.
[7] Ayşe Kadıoğlu, *Cumhuriyet Iradesi, Demokrasi Muhakemesi : Türkiye'de Demokratik Açılım Arayışları* (Metis Yayınları, 1999), http://www.metiskitap.com/catalog/book/4315.

order to exist. Today, it is very difficult to exist as a scholar who thinks intellectual conflict is good for the survival of differences; and rather than eliminating such differences, it is important to agree on how to disagree. Today, this is a minority position in Turkey and in a world where the self-righteousness of true believers (whether they are religious and/or nationalist) prevails. It is that space that is in need of recovery today. Towards that end, it is important to continue international academic collaborations and engage in solidarity with colleagues without falling into the trap of seeing them only as victims to be pitied for they are trying to survive this ordeal in dignity. It is important to continue to value their scholarship. A respectful gaze rather than pity is needed by scholars who are struggling for academic freedom.

What Is Academic Freedom? Perspectives from New York and Abu Dhabi —— *Catharine R. Stimpson*

—— *Catharine R. Stimpson is Graduate Dean Emerita and University Professor at New York University*

Let me begin with a historical allusion. In 387 BCE, the philosopher Plato founded a research and teaching center. He located it in a donated grove of trees, a garden, in what was then a suburb of Athens. The donor's name flowed over into the name of Plato's school, the "Academy," and into the rubric for the activities of higher education, "Academia." Among Plato's pupils was Aristotle, who went on to found his own center, the Lyceum. In 86 BCE, a Roman general, Sulla, pillaged the Lyceum. Centuries later, in 529 CE, after Christianity had become the official state religion of the Western and Eastern branches of the old Roman Empire, the emperor of Byzantium, Justinian, closed Plato's academy. He was suppressing "pagan" schools, books, and icons.

In brief, the history of religious and state control of inquiry is long and deep. As Jonathan R. Cole has written: "The defense of academic freedom is never easy."[1] Seeking control, authorities and institutions have many weapons at their command, so many that self-censorship can seem to

---

[1] Jonathan R. Cole, "Academic Freedom under Fire," in *Who's Afraid of Academic Freedom?*, ed. Akeel Bilgrami and Jonathan R. Cole (New York: Columbia University Press, 2015), 15.

be a prudent response to one's looming censors. Authorities can strip individuals of their passports, visas, rights to speech on any media, livelihoods, freedoms, and life itself. Authorities can strip institutions of their money (that power of the purse), accreditation (that power of the license), physical security (that power of violence and force), and legal identity (that power of dissolution). As a mechanism of control, states can decide when to enforce certain laws or when to let violations slip. They have the ability to structure uncertainty into their governance and to keep academics or journalists or artists or any oppositional figure off balance. However, a certainty remains: books can go up in flames; the internet can go down in the prison house of silence.

The fears of academic freedom are lively and numerous. If potentially freedom gives voice to error, it can disrupt "good order." Potentially "treasonous," it can be a danger to the authority of the state. Potentially "blasphemous," it can be a danger to a faith. Then, its intellectual errors are moral errors. I have greater sympathy with another ancient and modern fear: that it corrupts the young. Most parents of students love their children and understandably ask what might happen to them and to the values of their family in a free-wheeling classroom. The growth of higher education, its "massification," has brought many more students with families, and their "family values," into classrooms.

Yet, the resistance to the control is equally deep and far more creative. For the resistance affirms rather than negates human potential. I was an adolescent when I learned that Galileo (1564-1642) was a hero. For he saw reality anew and afresh. Although his thought was suppressed, history vindicated him as a founder of modern science. I was an undergraduate in a liberal arts college for women when I read Plato and Aristotle, without fear and with much favor. As a tenured professor in an American research university, I am the privileged beneficiary of the struggle that has installed academic freedom as a bedrock, often legally protected, principle of the modern university. As Cole also writes, " (...) freedom of inquiry is our reason for being."[2]

Because I teach for two months each spring at New York University Abu Dhabi, which celebrated its fourth graduation in May 2017, I have assumed that I am to comment on the Gulf States. On my office door in Abu Dhabi is a blue and white poster, with the declaration, in Hungarian and English, "I stand with CEU." I am an outsider, a non-expert participant-observer of higher education in the Gulf, one who is far more conversant with my home country, the United States. Limited though I am, I suggest that we first rehearse again, no matter how briefly, a complex argument about the limits of academic freedom.

The now-classical theory about academic freedom concerns the freedom of academics as academics. As academics, they occupy a special place and space, that of rational thought and inquiry. At the risk of being misunderstood, let me remind us of a famous statement by Kant. In 1784, he was under the comparatively benign rule of Frederick the Great, then alive but to die in 1786. Kant wrote, "Only one prince in the world says, 'Argue as much as you will, about what you will, but obey.'"[3] Since the late 19th and all of the 20th century, statements defining the classical theory of academic freedom and its boundaries abound. Among them is:

[2] Ibid., 55.
[3] Kant, *The Conflict of the Faculties (Der Streit Der Fakultäten)*, 221.

Freedom of teaching and discussion, freedom in carrying out research and disseminating and publishing the results thereof, freedom to express freely opinions about the academic institution or system in which one works, freedom from institutional censorship and freedom to participate in professional or representative academic bodies.[4]

Supporters of this classical theory also correctly realize that they should justify their freedom by demonstrating how they serve society, in time present and future. Dissent fuels well-being and progress. a pragmatic example: if you shut down the universities in Venezuela, you will destroy the next generation of doctors. Nor is academic freedom absolute. Another pragmatic example: defenders of academic freedom cannot condone such disrespectful behaviors as coercing students into a fawning acceptance of a teacher's prattlings.

Logically, the classical theory of academic freedom includes a belief in a high degree of institutional autonomy. a university must be able to make academic decisions and shape its identity as a place of teaching, research, and service. How bizarre, how unproductive, how wrong it would be for a professor to speak and write under the protection of academic freedom - only to have a minister of education unilaterally fire that professor at the minister's whim and will.

Yet, the norms of modern democracies and global human rights have gained some greater traction. They include the freedom of expression and association. I was a schoolchild in 1948 when the UN General Assembly "adopted and proclaimed" the Universal Declaration of Human Rights. Article 18 reads:

---

[4] UNESCO, "Recommendation Concerning the Status of Higher-Education Teaching Personnel" (1997), http://portal.unesco.org/en/ev.php-URL_ID=13144&URL_DO=DO_TOPIC&URL_SECTION=201.html.

Everyone has the right to freedom of thought, conscience and religion; this right includes freedom to change his religion or belief, and freedom, either alone or in community with others and in public or private, to manifest his religion or belief in teaching, practice, worship and observance.

Following it is Article 19:

Everyone has the right to freedom of opinion and expression; this right includes freedom to hold opinions without interference and to seek, receive and impart information and ideas through any media and regardless of frontiers.

As a result of this evolution, academics can now speak as citizens. Their identity has become a dual one: they are professional academics, and they are professional academics who are political citizens. What the rights of citizens are and what they ought to be is one of the disputed, defining bloodier questions of our time.

The American literary scholar David Bromwich is one proponent of this position. He writes:

(...) the limits of academic freedom should not be narrower than the limits of intellectual freedom (...) It is the right of the scholar to think, write, and speak whatever he or she wants to think, write, and speak (...) Understood in its broad and libertarian sense, academic freedom is a category of political freedom.[5]

---

[5] David Bromwich, "Academic Freedom and Its Opponents," in *Who's Afraid of Academic Freedom?*, ed. Akeel Bilgrami and Jonathan R. Cole (New York: Columbia University Press, 2015), 27.

In contrast, he declares, with a tinge of sarcasm, this is the position of his opposition.

> You are free (...) to say whatever you think within your
> discipline, by virtue of the license conferred by disciplinary
> training and the possession of a corresponding expertise
> (...) So long (...) as you go on producing knowledge (...) you
> retain the right to make whatever assertions you please.
> But when you step out of the bounds of your productive
> province, you forfeit all protection.[6]

Contrary to the stereotypes that I have heard expressed with irritating frequency, the Gulf States are highly diverse amongst and within themselves. The seven emirates of the United Arab Emirates (UAE) are different from each other. Abu Dhabi is not Dubai. The Emirates are not Saudi Arabia. If I might overgeneralize, I would say that they are the legatees of ancient and invaluable civilizations, but they are comparatively recent modern states that have ruling families. These states have often evolved out of political relations with Great Britain and the dynamics of these families. The Kingdom of Saudi Arabia was formed in 1932; Kuwait in 1961; Qatar, Bahrain, and the United Arab Emirates in 1971. They may have a high proportion of ex-patriate workers and inhabitants, about 90% in the UAE, who are not citizens. The Gulf States are also Muslim.

In May 1981, in Saudi Arabia, six of the Gulf States formed the Gulf Co-operation Council (GCC). They were Saudi Arabia, Kuwait, the UAE, Qatar, Bahrain, and Oman. The GCC charter speaks of "special relations, common characteristics and similar systems founded on the creed of Islam." The charter also describes a great purpose of the GCC as the formulation of "similar regulations" in "Economic and financial affairs/Commerce, customs and communications/Education and culture." Like the Middle

[6] Ibid., 31.

East as a whole, higher education has grown tremendously. In the entire region, university enrollment is up by nearly 50% in the last 10 years. 97% of the universities in the Arab world were created after 1950; 70% of those did not exist in 1991.[7] The rise of higher education is one sign of the states' capacity for change.

Recently, for at least three reasons, the conditions in the Gulf States, and by extension for higher education and academic freedom, have become even more complicated. One, well-known, is economic, the price of oil, the revenues of which fund such public goods as education. The second, also well-known and destructive, is the war in Yemen, which many analyze as a proxy struggle between the regional rivals of Iran and Saudi Arabia. Some specific results include attacks on campus protesters, campus bombings, and the occupation and closure of campuses. a branch of ISIS reportedly threatened students at the University of Aden with bombings if the campus did not become sex-segregated, ban music, and hold collective student prayer. War enables the state to crush dissent in the name of the flag and national security.

The third reason is very recent. On June 5, three members of the GCC (Saudi Arabia, the UAE, and Bahrain) blockaded a fourth member (Qatar). Egypt, and then other states, joined them. The President of the United States, Donald J. Trump, ferociously supported them - even if not all the members of his cabinet did. The ostensible motive for this dramatic "special relations"- shattering move against Qatar is its support of terrorism. In the UAE, the attorney general wrote of Doha's hostility and recklessness. In order to protect UAE national security, its interests, and its public, he ordered that any show of "(...) sympathy on social media or by any other means of communication is a cybercrime punishable by law."

---

[7] Scholars at Risk Network, "Universities in a Dangerous World: Defending Higher Education Communities and Values," 2016, https://www.scholarsatrisk.org/wp-content/uploads/2016/10/SAR-2016-Global-Congress-Report.pdf.

Offenses could lead to fines of Dh 500,000 or prison sentences of three to 15 years.[8] Other consequences for academic freedom and educational institutions are unclear, but as I speak, there are some reports of difficulties for non-Qatari students and faculty in Qatar or Qatari students in Bahrain, Saudi Arabia, or the UAE.[9]

Even before the June 5 actions, Lisa Anderson, a highly respected and experienced scholar of the Middle East, could say, "There is much worry about academic freedom in the Arab world."[10] One organization that monitors and documents violations against academic freedom, and protests against them, is Scholars at Risk (SAR). Founded in 2000, hosted at New York University, it is a global network of nearly 500 higher education institutions. SAR is concerned with academic freedom both in its classical sense and in its more recent connection to human rights. It protects threatened scholars, helping to find positions for them if they must go into exile or become refugees. SAR also serves as an advocate for academic values. Since its founding, SAR has had over 2,600 requests for assistance from nearly 130 countries. The largest percentages are from the Middle East and North Africa, with the most distressing of increases from Syria and Turkey. Sub-Saharan Africa and South Asia follow. With sorrow, we are also following Venezuela, where social institutions, including education, are collapsing.

SAR now publishes an annual report, Free to Think, a product of our Academic Freedom Monitoring Project. In our 2016 issue, we described 158 attacks on academic freedom in 35 countries—from travel restrictions

[8] Thamer Al Subaihi, "Supporting Qatar on Social Media a Cybercrime, Says UAE Attorney General," *The National*, June 7, 2017, https://www.thenational.ae/uae/supporting-qatar-on-social-media-a-cybercrime-says-uae-attorney-general-1.31515.

[9] Aisha Elgayar, "Arab Students Caught in Regional Conflict With Qatar," *Al-Fanar Media*, June 13, 2017, https://www.al-fanarmedia.org/2017/06/arab-students-caught-regional-conflict-qatar/.

[10] Scholars at Risk Network, "Universities in a Dangerous World: Defending Higher Education Communities and Values."

to killings, violence, and disappearances.[11] Of them, only 2 are in the Gulf (Kuwait, the UAE). The reports from Turkey and Egypt far outnumber those from the Gulf States. However, SAR's current concerns in the Gulf, which include difficulties before 2016, include some denials of entry into a country for academic purpose and four imprisonments, where we also fear for the physical health of our scholars. Three of them are in Bahrain, all in the STEM disciplines; one is in the UAE, in Economics.

The Gulf States are no more immune to the contours of the modern university and to the new technologies of information than any other region. For example, the UAE Constitution/Basic Law, written in 1971 and made permanent in 1996, has a preamble that calls for a gradual

> (…) dignified and free constitutional life, and progressing by steps towards a comprehensive, representative, democratic regime in an Islamic and Arab society free from fear and anxiety (…).

Part III, Article 30 then states that

> Freedom of opinion and expressing it verbally, in writing or by other means of expression shall be guaranteed within the limits of law.

Yet, "the law," when promulgated, can demand respect for the symbols of the UAE, its laws, religion, rulers, ruling families, and government.

In my experience, some universities might exercise a limited version of classical academic freedom. a recent faculty handbook in a major public

[11] Scholars at Risk, "Free to Think: Report of the Scholars at Risk Academic Freedom Monitoring Project," 2016, https://www.scholarsatrisk.org/wp-content/uploads/2016/11/Free_to_Think_2016.pdf.

institution in the UAE, Zayed University, calls for a balance between academic freedom and "students' sensibilities and (...) national cultural context." It writes of a "cultural and legal environment (that) is characterized by the imperative to be respectful of Islam, as well as all social groups." In a suggestive comment, it also draws a comparison between itself and "faith-based institutions in the United States."[12] Another accommodation is to create enclaves of academic freedom in public and private institutions. An enclave is a space that is carved out, with varying degrees of protection and varying arrangements, in which certain freedoms can be exercised or entertained.

A prominent example of an enclave is near Jeddah in Saudi Arabia, the King Abdullah University of Science and Technology (KAUST), a co-educational graduate university founded in 2009. Reading a recent KAUST "Faculty Handbook,"[13] I felt often an eerie similarity to one that an American research university might issue. Arguably, it is superficially easier to support academic freedom in science and technology than in the humanities and social sciences. Other examples might be the "American" universities or the branch campuses of American universities, for example, those in Education City in Qatar.

The enclave with which I am most familiar is New York University Abu Dhabi, a United States liberal arts research university. Significantly, the Emirate set up both traditional universities and two other models of Western education at about the same time: a branch of the Sorbonne, and the Masdar Institute of Science and Technology, associated with MIT. The agreement between the government of Abu Dhabi and New York University guarantees academic freedom on campus. That is to the great

[12] Office of the Provost, "Zayed University Faculty Handbook," 2009, http://www.zu.ac.ae/main/files/contents/edu/docs/accr/faculty_handbook.pdf.
[13] King Abdullah University of Science and Technology, "Faculty Handbook," 2015, https://academicaffairs.kaust.edu.sa/faculty-affairs/Documents/Faculty Handbook 2015-16 (updated 22 Mar 2016).pdf.

credit of the government. Although the university is not in the socially re-laxed precincts of Greenwich Village, and although it has made mistakes, I have never felt any violation of that agreement. I am, however, a tran-sient, an admitted visitor with a syllabus, in Abu Dhabi. I am not a politi-cal citizen of the UAE. Nor do I pretend to be. I am a political citizen of the United States, a feminist, a believer in LGBTQ rights, a civil libertarian, and a beneficiary of the United States Constitution and Bill of Rights. I have a dual identity and responsibilities.

I teach a course on "Law and the Imagination" to wonderful undergrad-uates from about 110 countries, some of them from deeply authoritarian and repressive and violent regimes. For many of them, the campus is a respite. We begin with "The Code of Hammurabi," parts of "Exodus" and Sophocles' "Antigone." We end with the "Universal Declaration of Human Rights." I have excellent colleagues. I have witnessed them do work of real value within the enclave that has effects outside of it. The colleagues I most admire are vigilant about academic freedom and about them-selves. They are wary about being cultural imperialists or self-righteous prigs. They also refuse to delude themselves about the tensions of living within an enclave. They are smart, have humility, and are, willing to admit error. In other words, they are genuine scholars.

To be too succinct: when I teach at New York University Abu Dhabi, I am grateful for the classical theory of academic freedom. When I speak as a United States citizen, I am grateful for modern theories of human rights. Given the number of authoritarian governments in the world, be they secular or religious, academic freedom needs both theories in active practice in order to flourish.

No matter how imperfectly, I am also aware of the realities of visions, of faiths, of aesthetic worlds, of cognitive dissonance, of the malleability of ideas and information, of passions, and of appetites. I do, after all, study literature. However, Plato was one of my tutors about reason. When I first encountered "The Phaedrus," I gained the ancient metaphor of the Charioteer in his sweaty, intense struggle by and for reason. The same liberal arts college that gave me Plato also gave me Kant, not that I understood him. However, I can return to him and to The Contest of the Faculties. He writes:

> Now the power to judge autonomously—that is, freely (according to principles of thought in general) is called reason. So, the philosophy faculty, because it must answer for the truth of the teachings it is to adopt or even allow, must be conceived as free and subject only to laws given by reason, not by the government.[14]

Whether on the large globe or in the smallest, dustiest university, our belief in academic freedom, and our defense of it, is nothing less than our subscription to reason itself.

[14] Kant, *The Conflict of the Faculties (Der Streit Der Fakultäten)*.

THE THREAT WITHIN:
THE STRUGGLE FOR AND AGAINST
ACADEMIC FREEDOM WITHIN U.S.
UNIVERSITIES

The Fundamental Role of Academic Freedom and Free Inquiry in US Higher Education
—— *Jonathan R. Cole*

—— *Jonathan R. Cole is the John Mitchell Mason Professor of Columbia University and was its Provost and Dean of the Faculties from 1989–2003. He is a member of the CEU Board of Trustees.*

Academic Freedom and Attacks against it in the US from a Historical Perspective

I want to begin with an assertion, which I believe is supported by facts: You cannot have a truly great university without a deep commitment to the institutionalization and adherence to academic freedom and free inquiry. Below I illustrate a hierarchy of core values of universities. You will notice at the very foundation of that hierarchy are two fundamental enabling values: trust, and academic freedom and free inquiry. These are enabling because, without them, I don't believe you can achieve meritocracy and some of the other values which are in the hierarchy itself. Academic freedom and trust are at the very core of what we do; at the heart of our existence in creating and transmitting knowledge.

Academic freedom is an enabling value

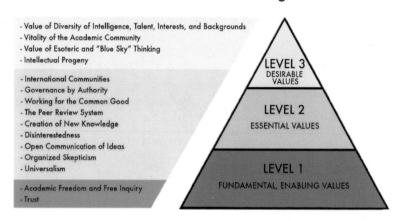

Figure 1. Source: Jonathan R. Cole, *Toward a More Perfect University*
(Public Affairs, 2016).

I also want to note that attacks on academic freedom are not new, certainly in the United States. From the very beginning of the turn of the 20th century, we had the attacks and firing of the distinguished economist and sociologist, E. A. Ross at Stanford, who was critical of Leyland Stanford as a railroad magnate and for his views on eugenics. There were an enormous number of firings related to faculty members' opposition to conscription prior and during World War I, as well as their responses to the passage of the Alien and Sedition Acts. Nicholas Murray Butler, Columbia University's president, asserted in his 1917 Commencement address that there isn't going to be any tolerance or questioning of the American entrance into the First World War:

Nicolas Murray
Butter

What had been tolerated before became intolerable now. What had been wrongheaded was now sedition. What had been folly was now treason. In your presence I speak for the whole University.... When I say... that there will be no place at Columbia University, either on the rolls of its faculty or on the rolls of its students, for any person who opposes or who counsels opposition to the effective enforcement of the laws of the United States, or who acts, speaks or writes treason. The separation of such person from Columbia University will be as speedy as the discovery of the offense.

There were similar statements at the time made by the president of Cornell, Edmond Ezra Day:

(...) a man who belongs to the Communist Party and who follows the party line is thereby disqualified from participating in a free, honest inquiry after truth, and from belonging on a university faculty devoted to the search for truth.

Edmond Ezra Day

and by Yale's president, Charles Seymour:

There will be no witch hunts at Yale because there will be no witches. We do not intend to hire Communists.

Charles Seymour

Whether they were red scares, or the repression took some other form, academic freedom itself has been periodically under attack in the United States for over 100 years. During the McCarthy period and the Second Red Scare, great scientists like Linus Pauling, who won two Nobel prizes, and who might have won a third for the discovery of the structure of the DNA, had he not been hindered in that effort because he was being hounded by the FBI, while being denied the opportunity to go to England to accept membership in the Royal Society. Many people think he would have discovered the DNA structure before Watson and Crick.

The great defender of academic freedom was Robert Hutchins at the University of Chicago. He said during the Red Scare and the famous Illinois legislature's Broyles inquiries into communism on university campuses, especially at the University of Chicago:

The danger to our institutions is not from the tiny minority who do not believe in them. It is from those who would mistakenly repress the free spirit upon which those institutions are built (...) The policy of repression of ideas cannot work and has never worked. The alternative is the long, difficult road of education.
Robert Hutchins

In a further statement, Hutchins said that the problem with witch hunts was:

> (...) not how many professors would be fired for their beliefs, but how many think they might be. The entire teaching profession is intimidated.

He suggests that when you have apprehension and you scare professors because of threats to their freedom to express their views or pursue their research ideas, which may run contrary to the received wisdom, then you have the entire teaching profession intimidated and the concomitant effect of their refusal to take on new subjects and express contrarian ideas.

During all periods, be it the Vietnam War or the aftermath of 9/11, one can see attacks on aspects of free inquiry. For example, the Bush administration politicized the Center for Disease Control. During the post 9/11 period Congress tried (as it had before) to curtail peer review, and it tried to eliminate NSF funding of political science research that was not related to national defense. It made an effort to limit the publication of biological research that it thought could aid terrorist groups. The FBI searched scientists' laboratories. Currently, we see threats to eliminate the National Endowment of Humanities or the National Endowment for the Arts. In sum, there have been many dark periods over the past century where academic freedom and ideas of free inquiry have, in fact, been under attack.

Today, we can observe a disturbing new development: attacks that are coming from inside universities rather than from external authority. The unlikely source has been university students. Historically, students have by and large been expansionists for free expression and for tolerance of free inquiry. One can point to instances that are only vaguely related to academic freedom where students have protested work on campus: for example, the efforts by students during the Vietnam War to eliminate classified military research from university campuses. They succeeded in that protest. But today, many students are beginning to question the foundation of free inquiry and academic freedom at universities. These protests have taken the form of insisting that campus speakers with opprobrious points of view not be permitted to speak on campus, that faculty should provide "trigger warnings" when teaching books that could be offensive to some subgroup of the university community, that universities should disinvite Commencement speakers from giving talks on campus, and that professors should be limited in what they can discuss in their classrooms. Universities are called upon to provide "safe intellectual spaces" for vulnerable students, and universities are being pushed to take punitive action against what some students perceive to be "microaggressions." To be sure, academic freedom requires physical safe spaces for discourse to take place, but it also requires that we respect various points of view among speakers, even when the point of view is opprobrious to some.

Two fundamental sources of academic freedom in the US

The fundamental principles of academic freedom have been expressed well in two reports originating at The University of Chicago—separated by roughly a half-century. The first set comes from the 1967 Kalven Committee Report which is only three pages in length and yet powerfully lays out a few basic tenets about the university and academic freedom:

Herry Kalven

A university faithful to its mission will provide enduring challenges to social values, policies, practices, and institutions. By design and by effect, it is the institution which creates discontent with the existing social arrangements and proposes new ones. In brief, a good university, like Socrates, will be upsetting. (…) [It] must embrace, be hospitable to, and encourage the widest diversity of views within its own community. It is not a club, it is not a trade association, it is not a lobby. (…) The neutrality of the university as an institution arises then not from a lack of courage nor out of indifference and insensitivity. It arises out of respect for free inquiry and the obligation to cherish diversity of viewpoints.

I'm not sure that our students, when they enter the university today, have any concept that one of the missions of a great university is to confront their biases and presuppositions, to challenge them, not necessarily to have them abandon their ideas, but at least to learn how to defend them. Part of the Kalven Committee Report—which was produced during turbulent times—states that the university is a community, but one where nobody, including the rector, the president, or the trustees speak for the university. The University is a community of individuals. The idea is fundamentally not to encroach upon or intimidate the views of any minority in the community. Then the neutrality of the university arises out of courage.

Sixty years after the Kalven Committee Report, the University of Chicago published another report on free expression, which I shall call the Stone Committee Report since Professor of law and former Chicago Provost Geoffrey Stone chaired the committee. Finally, I'll end with a statement by John Etchemendy, the longtime provost of Stanford University. The short Chicago document lays out the role of free expression on campuses, expression that is closely linked to academic freedom:

Geoffrey Stone

(...) it is not the proper role of the University to attempt to shield individuals from ideas and opinions they find unwelcome, disagreeable, or even deeply offensive. Although the University greatly values civility, and although all members of the University community share in the responsibility for maintaining a climate of mutual respect, concerns about civility and mutual respect can never be used as a justification for closing off discussion of ideas, however offensive or disagreeable those ideas may be to some members of the community.

If that is the position at the University of Chicago, it may not be the rule at other institutions of higher learning. However, John Etchemendy, the outgoing Provost of Stanford University, in a talk to Stanford Trustees, reinforces the concerns of the Stone Committee Report:

John Etchemendy

I am actually more worried about the threat [to the university] from within. Over the years, I have watched a growing intolerance at universities in this country—not intolerance along racial or ethnic or gender lines— there, we have made laudable progress. Rather, a kind of intellectual intolerance, a political one-sidedness, that is the antithesis of what universities should stand for. It manifests itself in many ways: in the intellectual monocultures that have taken over certain disciplines; in the demands to disinvite speakers and outlaw groups whose views we find offensive; in constant calls for the university itself to take political stands. We decry certain news outlets as echo chambers, while we fail to notice the echo chamber we've built around ourselves

The speakers at this conference consider these principles and discuss whether or not they go too far.

Lessons from Middlebury —— *Allison Stanger*

—— *Allison Stanger is Russell J. Leng '60 Professor of International Politics and Economics at Middlebury College*

Introduction

Traveling to the Academic Freedom conference, I enjoyed landing at a Budapest airport named for Franz Liszt. Later this week—in fact, tomorrow—I will touch down at Prague's Vaclav Havel International Airport. I want to begin by holding up these relatively new names (2011 and 2012, respectively) as an occasion for celebration. Could there be anything better for a lover of the arts and sciences?

I visited Budapest for the first time in 1983. My first trip to Prague was in 1986. Both cities were then very different places. Though we seem to have returned to a dark hour in human history, it should give us all strength to remember that most of us gathered here have been fortunate witnesses to Central Europe's rebirth. The lands of Beethoven, Mozart, Freud, Kafka, Musil, Haydn, Kertész, and von Neumann clearly have unlimited future potential.

Academic freedom is a foundation for both knowledge and human excellence. It matters what is happening in universities, because democracy and liberal education are intertwined, as Joan Scott has so eloquently argued. I'll confine my remarks to what I have learned over the past few months through my own personal experience. It won't be scientific. I will not provide data. But perhaps some of my conjectures might be tested against those of others writing in this volume, sparking meaningful dialogue about what we value most.

The fragility of things most Americans take for granted is something I only recently came to know. Important values I took to be self-evident truths are currently facing the gravest of challenges within the Ivory Tower as well as beyond its confines, and that challenge is global.

The Middlebury Incident

Student protesters disrupt speaker Charles Murray
on March 2 at McCullough Student Center, Middlebury College
(source: http://www.middlebury.edu)

Let me elaborate a bit on what happened to me this spring. Several of my students asked me to moderate a talk with the American Enterprise scholar Charles Murray. For those who don't know him, Charles Murray wrote a controversial book almost 25 years ago called *The Bell Curve*, which is what whipped students and faculty alike into a frenzy at the prospect of him speaking on campus. Although he was coming to talk about his 2012 book *Coming Apart*, which explores polarization in the United States and pretty much foresaw the election of Donald Trump, that fact was not significant to the protesters. They were stuck on what he was said to have written over two decades ago.

When my students asked me to engage with Dr. Murray by asking the first three or four questions, I agreed without giving it much thought. My students know I'm a Democrat, but the college courses I teach are obviously non-partisan. I have a PhD in political science. I don't need to tell you that academia is overwhelmingly left-leaning. In that context, it is especially important for any serious political science department to engage the full spectrum of political views. That is why Middlebury's political science department co-sponsored the Charles Murray event. That is also why the American Political Science Association (APSA) publicly condemned the violence at Middlebury College, which "undermined the ability of faculty and students to engage in the free exchange of ideas and debate, thereby impeding academic freedom on the Middlebury campus."[1]

As I subsequently wrote in the *New York Times*, I thought that asking Charles Murray challenging questions was an opportunity to demonstrate publicly my commitment to the free and fair exchange of ideas in my classroom.[2] But as some of you may already know, Dr. Murray was drowned out by students who never let him speak, we were forced to retreat to another location to livestream our conversation, and he and I were intimidated and physically assaulted while trying to leave cam-

---

[1] APSA, "Statement on Violence at Middlebury College on March 2," 2017, http://www.apsanet.org/Portals/54/goverance/2017/APSA Statement on Violence at Middlebury College on March 2.pdf?ver=2017-03-09-102506-453.

[2] Allison Stanger, "Understanding the Angry Mob at Middlebury That Gave Me a Concussion," *New York Times*, https://www.nytimes.com/2017/08/16/us/after-charlottesville-violence-colleges-brace-for-more-clashes.html, March 13, 2017.

pus. Charles Murray was 74 years old at the time. When I saw him being attacked, I did what any decent human being would do in those circumstances. I took his arm so that he would not fall, and that is when the hatred turned on me.

So why did this happen in the United States of America, the land of the free? I have had ample opportunity to reflect on this question, and I think there are three principal reasons for it. First, the election of Donald Trump set the stage for over-reaction and misinterpretation. In that milieu, Charles Murray became a lightning rod that he might not otherwise have been. Second, in the run-up to the talk, some members of the Middlebury faculty cheered on the protests and did not encourage their students to read Charles Murray, or listen to him first, before drawing their own conclusions about his work and his character. I can't stress to you enough how significant that was for the events that followed. We had Middlebury faculty members acknowledging publicly that they had never read anything that Charles Murray had written, but because they had read a collection of pull quotes on the Southern Poverty Law Center website, they knew that Murray should not be speaking on campus.[3] Third, some students believed that shutting down speech was a means to social justice. And some Middlebury professors shared that view, thereby encouraging radical action.

In the days that followed my injury, a campus consensus seemingly emerged that the goals of inclusivity and freedom of expression were in

---

[3] Interestingly, in the aftermath of the Middlebury mayhem, President of the Southern Poverty Law Center Richard Cohen argued publicly against shutting down speech on college campuses. He told the New York Times in August 2017, "We might want to shame them, or think they are sick, but students have a right to listen to who they want to listen to, and we don't have the right to censor that... Don't give these fools an audience."

See: Dana Goldstein, "After Charlottesville Violence, Colleges Brace for More Clashes," New York Times, August 16, 2017, https://www.nytimes.com/2017/08/16/us/after-charlottesville-violence-colleges-brace-for-more-clashes.html.

direct conflict. Middlebury's President Laurie Patton, thankfully, challenged this view. As she elaborated in a *Wall Street Journal* opinion piece in June 2017, nothing could be further from the truth, since free expression is the means to greater diversity.[4] Yet the view that inclusivity and free speech are mutually exclusive had and will continue to have popular appeal, since it seems to embrace moderation. It comforted those pained by the conflict they were witnessing, both on campus and beyond, because it meant that one didn't have to choose a side. Instead, one could stake out what seemed to be a middle position and thereby avoid conflict. One should not mistake this silence for a majority endorsement of shutting down speech. Rather, a very vocal and radical minority successfully preempted the emergence of any moderate consensus at Middlebury in spring 2017.[5]

There were quite a few brave souls, however, who immediately saw the foundation of the university under challenge and spoke out publicly. They organized a Principles of Free Expression petition that garnered over 100 signatures from Middlebury faculty and was published in the *Wall Street Journal* in March 2017.[6] I noticed three general patterns among the signatories. First, many supporters had studied or experienced intellectual life under an authoritarian or totalitarian regime. Second, many of the signatories had lived in American red states and had loved ones with whom they disagreed politically. And finally, quite a few of the signatories were older rather than younger. Now I myself happen to fall into all three

---

[4] Laurie L. Patton, "The Right Way to Protect Free Speech on Campus - WSJ," *The Wall Street Jounral*, June 6, 2017, https://www.wsj.com/articles/the-right-way-to-protect-free-speech-on-campus-1497019583.
[5] AAllison Stanger, "Middlebury, My Divided Campus," https://www.nytimes.com/2017/04/03/education/edlife/middlebury-divided-campus-charles-murray-free-speech.html, *New York Times*, April 3, 2017.
[6] Jay Parini and Keegan Callanan, "Middlebury's Statement of Principle," *The Wall Street Journal*, March 6, 2017, https://www.wsj.com/articles/middleburys-statement-of-principle-1488846993.
and
Free Inquiry on Campus, "Free Inquiry on Campus: a Statement of Principles by over One Hundred Middlebury College Professors," 2017, https://freeinquiryblog.wordpress.com/.

of these categories. I should also add that professors from the sciences, mathematics, religion, and philosophy were disproportionately represented. In general, the signatories understood the critical importance of being able to agree to disagree, both for the sake of the community, free inquiry and even democracy itself. It was shocking to discover that I had colleagues who did not share our understanding of the academy's and America's core values.[7]

How can we explain this conflict within the American academy? How is it possible for intellectuals in a free society to embrace censorship as an acceptable means? The short answer is that the proponents of shutting down speech or frightening off speakers don't see themselves as censors. They see themselves as upholding free speech by righting power inequities. Settling scores with someone like Charles Murray constitutes social justice.

The best articulated version of this position comes from New York University's Vice-Provost for Faculty, Arts, Humanities and Diversity Ulrich Baer. In an April 2017 *New York Times* opinion piece titled "What snowflakes get right about free speech," Baer deploys the French post-structuralist philosopher Jean-François Lyotard in arguing "that some topics, such as claims that some human beings are by definition inferior to others, or illegal or unworthy of legal standing, are not open to debate because such people cannot debate them on the same terms." Baer supports censorship and argues that free speech absolutists are the real censors in that they challenge the rights of minorities to participate in public discourse. Baer is therefore not "overly worried that even the shrillest heckler's veto will end free speech in America."[8] In other words, Charles Murray and I deserved to be shouted down.

---

[7] For more on the Middlebury campus divide, see: Stanger, "Middlebury, My Divided Campus."

[8] Ulrich Baer, "What 'Snowflakes' Get Right About Free Speech," *The New York Times*, April 24, 2017, https://www.nytimes.com/2017/04/24/opinion/what-liberal-snowflakes-get-right-about-free-speech.html.

As I am still suffering from a heckler's veto concussion, I am perhaps not the best person to pronounce this line of reasoning specious. But I will note here that for those who have experienced life under communist or fascist dictatorship, it is an all too familiar argument. It is a position where ideology and groupthink call the shots, where harm to other humans is construed as collateral damage. As Vaclav Havel argued in his powerful 1978 essay, "The Power of the Powerless," ideology is "a specious way of relating to the world. It offers human beings the illusion of an identity, of dignity, and of morality while making it easier for them to part with them."[9]

After Donald Trump's election, there is a dangerous idea taking hold on the American left that one must fight fire with fire. As a result, we now have an Alt-Left and an Alt-Right in the United States. The Alt-Left has embraced extremism in what they perceive as the only way to respond to Alt-Right extremism. In resisting Trumpism, they essentially advocate using Trump tactics. Democracy and reasoned debate have been and will be the main casualties, since the extreme left and extreme right are rebelling against liberalism itself. In this context, upholding freedom of expression protects all of us, because it gives individuals ways to dissent without resorting to violence.

Central Europeans should know better. a divided left is precisely what enabled the Nazi revolution. Retaliatory laws from both left and right that undermine freedom of expression, assembly, and speech must be denounced, both here and in the United States. Germany learned from its mistakes and got this balance right after a totalitarian past. Hungary must do the same. And in so doing, Americans will continue to have much to learn from Central Europe.

Thank you.

---

[9] Vaclav Havel, "The Power of the Powerless," *http://www.vaclavhavel.cz*, 1978, http:// www.vaclavhavel.cz/showtrans.php?cat=eseje&val=2_aj_eseje.html&typ=HTML.

Academic Freedom and Controversial Speech about Campus Governance —— *Rogers Brubaker*

—— *Rogers Brubaker is Professor of Sociology, University of California, Los Angeles and UCLA Foundation Chair; Visiting Professor, CEU.*

Classical definitions of academic freedom focused on freedom of research and teaching. In the American context, the right of professors to speak freely as citizens outside the university has also been emphasized. But many recent controversies over academic freedom in the US—and I limit my comments to the US—have turned on speech inside the university yet outside the traditional domains of research and teaching.

Research and teaching continue of course to be central to the defense of academic freedom in the face of external pressures, notably from private and public funders, government regulators, and the populist right. But I have been asked to address *internal* threats to academic freedom. And while some internal controversies have focused on the freedom of research and teaching, many have focused on other issues.

The most widely discussed of these controversies have concerned invitations to controversial outside speakers. Public attention has focused on efforts by the campus left to "disinvite" or "de-platform" speakers such as Charles Murray at Middlebury and Milo Yiannopoulos and Ann Coulter at Berkeley. These widely publicized incidents have already generated a substantial backlash: several conservative state legislatures have passed campus speech bills.[1] The campus right has also sought to prevent or disrupt events involving controversial (especially pro-Palestinian) outside speakers.

But there is another kind of internal academic freedom controversy that I would like to highlight. This concerns the freedom to speak out about issues of campus governance. Consider three recent examples.

In March 2015, students at Northwestern marched carrying mattresses and pillows to protest an article by Professor Laura Kipnis, an outspoken feminist cultural critic. *The Chronicle of Higher Education* article criticized new institutional rules regulating intimate relationships between faculty and students and skewered what Kipnis called the mood of "sexual paranoia" on college campuses.[2] Students petitioned the administration for an "official condemnation" of the article. Subsequently, two students filed formal title IX complaints against Kipnis on the basis of the article.[3] This triggered a prolonged, quasi-judicial official investigation that eventually exonerated Kipnis.

Later that year, Nicholas and Erica Christakis, the heads of one of Yale's residential colleges, were the targets of massive student protests calling for their dismissal. The trigger was an email Erica Christakis wrote reflecting critically—but in a thoughtful, low-key way—on an earlier email that had been sent by Yale's Intercultural Affairs Counsel to all Yale students. The earlier email had called on students to avoid "culturally unaware or

[1] Conor Friedersdorf, "The Campus-Speech Debate Spends Summer Break in Statehouses," *The Atlantic*, September 3, 2017, https://www.theatlantic.com/politics/archive/2017/08/the-campus-speech-debate-is-summering-in-statehouses/535608/.
[2] Laura Kipnis, "Sexual Paranoia Strikes Academe," *The Chronicle of Higher Education*, February 27, 2015, http://www.chronicle.com/article/Sexual-Paranoia-Strikes/190351.
[3] "My Title IX Inquisition," *The Chronicle of Higher Education*, May 29, 2015, http://www.chronicle.com/article/My-Title-IX-Inquisition/230489.

Students carry mattresses and pillows to protest Professor Kipnis' opinion piece. Illustration added by the editors, not the author

(source: http://dailynorthwestern. com/2015/03/10/campus/students-carry-mattresses-pillows-to-protest-professors-controversial-article/)

insensitive choices" in their Halloween costumes and provided guidance for avoiding "cultural appropriation and/or misrepresentation." In response, Christakis acknowledged "genuine concerns about cultural and personal representation" but worried about universities becoming "places of censure and prohibition" and about the loss of confidence in students' capacity to regulate their own conduct without bureaucratic guidance from above.[4]

My last example concerns the protests that engulfed Evergreen State College in Washington in May 2017. Here too the trigger was an email, this one circulated by biology professor Bret Weinstein. Weinstein's email criticized an official invitation to "allies" of "people of color" to absent themselves from campus for a so-called "Day of Absence" in order to attend a full day of workshops and other events addressing "issues of race, equality, allyship, inclusion, and privilege" "from a majority culture or white perspective," while the same issues would be addressed "from the perspective of people of color" in a full day of on-campus pro-

---

[4] Christakis' email can be read at https://www.thefire.org/email-from-erika-christakis-dressing-yourselves-email-to-silliman-college-yale-students-on-halloween-costumes/

gramming. This was a new twist on a longstanding Evergreen tradition, originally inspired by a satirical 1965 play depicting the chaos that results when the white residents of a southern town must cope with the sudden disappearance of the town's black residents. In previous years, students, faculty, and staff of color had been invited to attend an off-campus program discussing such issues, while allies had been invited to discuss the issues at on-campus workshops. Weinstein supported this tradition, but objected to the reversal of format, which he interpreted as a call for white students, faculty, and staff to absent themselves from campus.[5] Weinstein had earlier criticized a plan to require an "equity justification" or explanation for all faculty hires on the grounds that it would "[subordinate] all other characteristics of applicants to one thing." Students demanded that Weinstein be fired; police advised Weinstein that it wasn't safe for him to remain on campus; and 50 Evergreen faculty members signed a letter calling for a formal "disciplinary investigation" against Weinstein after he went to the media to tell his side of the story.

Bret Weinstein ● @BretWeinstein · 4. Juni
Graffiti on Purce Hall. Purce was our last president. A leader, committed to the college.
Wouldn't have allowed chaos. Happens to be black.

Tweets by Bret Weinstein in the aftermath of the Evergreen College incident. The lower one, depicting Weinstein himself. Illustration added by the editors, not the author

(Source: https:// twitter.com/ BretWeinstein)

---

[5] Weinstein's email can be read at http://www.theolympian.com/news/politics-government/article153826004.html

Tweets by Bret Weinstein in the aftermath of the Evergreen College incident. The lower one, depicting Weinstein himself. Illustration added by the editors, not the author

(Source: https://twitter.com/BretWeinstein)

These controversies have several things in common. Unlike many other campus controversies, they originated not in a clash between the newly emboldened campus right and the left, or between liberals and conservatives, but in a clash between liberals and the identarian left. Each controversy began with the articulation of liberal reservations about self-consciously progressive policies or practices pursued in the name of fostering inclusiveness and diversity on campus. And in each case, protesters did not seek to argue with the liberal critiques; they sought instead to stigmatize, delegitimize, and punish those critiques, treating them as outside the bounds of legitimate discussion.

The calls for dismissal of the Christakises and Weinsteins and the launching of a formal disciplinary investigation against Kipnis are in my view strong grounds for including in formulations of academic freedom an explicit and unambiguous defense of the freedom to speak out about issues of campus governance. Such speech should not simply be constitutionally protected, but *institutionally* protected, that is, free from threats of internal sanction. a vibrant notion of academic freedom should defend the *legitimacy* of such speech, not simply its *legality*.

These controversies about campus governance reveal fundamental debates about the particular kind of institution the university is and should be. Should universities be defined as spaces of freewheeling "debate, discussion and even disagreement" that may "at times (...) challenge you and even cause discomfort"? This was the view taken by a much-discussed University of Chicago letter to incoming students last August.[6]

Or should colleges and universities be defined as spaces of mutual respect and recognition, where speech is and should be carefully practiced and regulated out of respect for the sensibilities of vulnerable groups, so as to create a more truly inclusive and egalitarian learning environment?

The goal of creating a more inclusive and egalitarian learning environment is a noble and important one. But pursuing this goal by policing speech and protecting feelings strikes me as misguided and dangerous, for three reasons.

First, the paternalistic, subjectivist, and therapeutic stance that informs this approach—a stance that treats students as fragile beings whose feelings must be protected—risks limiting and disabling those it is intended to serve. a one-sided focus on protecting and respecting feelings is arguably much more limiting than a focus on cultivating and respecting capacities.

Second, the paternalistic stance is embodied and expressed in an increasingly influential and institutionalized discourse built on the concept of cumulative and systematic micro-aggressions. This discourse redefines and inflates the notions of "violence," "trauma," "assault," and "safety" as well as "bias" and "discrimination"; it generates an ever-expanding cat-

[6] From a letter of Jay Ellison, Dean of Students if the University of Chicago, to the class of 2020 students: http://www.intellectualtakeout.org/sites/ito/files/acceptance_letter.jpg

alog of harms caused by speech acts; and it cultivates and nurtures ever more exquisite forms of sensitivity to such harms. Most crucially, it makes feelings the ultimate arbiter of whether a harm has occurred.

Third, the new campus paternalism makes everyone in the university community responsible for anticipating—and thereby avoiding—the possible harms that their speech might cause. Failure to avoid the harms caused by speech acts—however unintended those harms might be—may be grounds for subjecting the speaker to disciplinary action. The proliferation of formal disciplinary investigations—often with minimal or inadequate procedural protections for the accused—has received considerable attention in the domain of sexual harassment,[7] but investigatory bureaucracies have been expanding to other domains as well.

These tendencies point in an increasingly and disturbingly illiberal direction. They threaten to transform the university from a space of free and unencumbered exchange into a space of constrained, monitored, and inhibited exchange. They threaten to remake the university into a disciplinary institution in the Foucauldian sense, one that seeks—through an expanding array of training programs and through the proliferation and expansion of investigative and disciplinary bureaucracies—to produce docile subjects who will speak in institutionally correct ways.

But docile subjects are produced, most effectively, through anticipatory self-censorship. In a context in which harm has been redefined as subjective offense, in which everyone is obliged to anticipate the possible

---

[7] See the statement issued by 28 members of the Harvard Law School faculty, voicing concerns about the new sexual harassment policies and procedures adopted by Harvard in 2014:
Eugene Volokh, "28 Harvard Law Professors Condemn Harvard's New Sexual Harassment Policy and Procedures," *The Washington Post*, October 15, 2014, https://www.washingtonpost.com/news/volokh-conspiracy/wp/2014/10/15/28-harvard-law-professors-condemn-harvards-new-sexual-harassment-policy-and-procedures/?utm_term=.e7a4631bd6c0.

harms that their speech might cause to others, and in which that obligation is enforceable through formal and informal sanctions, self-policing and self-censorship become routine, and the exchange of ideas and opinions—in research, teaching, and discussions about campus governance—is restricted by the need to avoid any possibility of giving offense. This cannot help but have a massive chilling effect on campus speech.

What is to be done? This is a difficult question, especially in the present American context, where liberal visions of the university are threatened not only, or even especially, from within, but also by much more powerful forces without, especially corporatization, privatization, conservative state and federal legislatures, anti-intellectualist right-wing populism, and of course a newly energized Alt-Right. The question is complicated by the connection between the threat from within and the threat from without: needless to say, events like the Evergreen and Yale protests or the Berkeley and Middlebury disturbances are red meat for Breitbart, Fox News, and conservative state legislatures.

In this climate, it is difficult to find a space for a liberal critique. And liberal criticism of course risks being coopted by the right. Yet this is no reason for liberals to remain silent. As an unapologetic liberal, I believe liberals must become more visible and vocal in campus politics. I think we need to stand up and speak out on behalf of a liberal understanding of the university, rather than simply grumble privately about the slow erosion and marginalization of that understanding.

Academic Freedom in the US and Its Enemies: A Polemic ——— *Leon Botstein*

——— *Leon Botstein is President of Bard College and Chairman of the CEU Board of Trustees*

I would like to preface my remarks with an analogy to the interwar period. As you may know, there was a satirical but prophetic novel published in Vienna in 1922 by Hugo Bettauer called *Die Stadt ohne Juden*, 'The City without Jews'. It was a sharply drawn futuristic account of a Vienna purged of Jews. Bettauer's fantasy (which was turned into a movie) became reality in 1945. Bettauer described the most radical consequences of decades of Viennese political anti-Semitism so potently that he was assassinated by a self-professed Austrian Nazi in 1925.

My approach to the question of what is happening now on the American campus is framed by the tacit assumption that one could paint a futuristic picture of university life in the United States in which anything resembling academic freedom and the tolerance of reason and free expression would be absent. I project this nightmare as someone who is responsible for an institution in the United States and is worried every day that something terrible might happen on campus. The debate that rages now is not constructive. It is frightening. I'm not an expert in this field but I sense danger and I want to describe how that danger appears to me in four points.

The first point requires us to take sympathetically and seriously the (often younger) faculty and student critique in the United States of the principle and practice of free speech. Free speech is seen as a dated "liberal" ideological conspiracy maintained by powerful people, mostly white and older faculty, alumni and trustees, to maintain their power and sustain the university as an instrument of that power. The university is seen as allied with big business and with government, the primary sources of support for most universities, especially research universities. Free speech appears little more than the hypocritical moralistic conceit among those in control of the status quo, and is therefore a seemingly neutral ideal that supports a playing field that is not level in terms of race and class and is designed to keep everything in place just as it is.

Why would an intelligent, well-meaning young person believe such a claim in the United States of America? Let me begin by adducing a few reasons: Consider the radical inequality of wealth, the absolute visibility of excessive obscene wealth in the US, the persistence of poverty, under-employment and the evidence of racism in the north and in the south, and the scandalously high cost of tuition and limited access to university education. Despite all the progress made since the end of World War II, these factors are evident to anyone, particularly the post-Cold War generations. Add to that the vulgar, blatant, dismissive attitude towards women, immigrants, and citizens of color, encouraged by our new elected president. And then add to that the controversy that surrounds the rights of people of differing sexual identities and orientations. There is a kind of dissonance between the rhetoric of free expression and free play of ideas on the one hand and the seemingly recalcitrant reality of discrimination, intolerance and inequity. Somehow the wrong ideas always win. Somehow nothing changes, there is little progress despite all the rhetoric about the power of ideas to sort themselves out in a condition of freedom on behalf of truth and justice. This in part explains the level of anger which exists behind both the alt-right and the radical anti-fascist left movements.

My second point is that we must confront the distortion and appropriation of the anti-enlightenment academic discourse that flourished in the 1970s and 1980s. Today's activists, who contest the traditions of free speech have absorbed somewhere, out of the *ether,* a reductive version of the post-positivist epistemological critique of knowledge. They believe there is actually no knowledge and no truth, and no privileged frame of reference that approaches objectivity. Truth is all subjective, and emanates from the perspective of the viewer, rendering subjectivity, per se, legitimacy and authority. Someone told them a distorted fairy-tale about Einstein's special theory of relativity: that everything is ultimately relative, and that there is no truth. Newton may have believed in truth but modern science has debunked that. Wrong as this may be vis-a-vis Einstein and relativity, the bowdlerizing of modern physics, from Schrödinger's cat and Heisenberg's uncertainty principle to the frame of references in the special theory of relativity, ended up undermining the tools of reason, the principles of argument and the rules of evidence. Somehow the word got out, in no small measure courtesy of French structural theorists, that knowledge is a social construct, in which universal truths do not exist. The critics of free expression don't believe that there are rational grounds to distinguish right from wrong.

There is one glaring exception and that concerns the application of basic science. When it comes to being wheeled into an emergency room or getting on an airplane, the epistemological critique vanishes. No one gets on an airplane and says it is a conspiracy. Few choose to take on the task of creating a non-hegemonic, perhaps non-Western, not primarily

male-dominated alternative construct of air travel that is a sympathetically subjective, less loud, less noisy, less polluting mode of getting
across the ocean quickly. But there is a frighteningly large segment of educated individuals who believe false claims about vaccination, deny the
results of modern science regarding the treatment of disease and contest
the results of climate science. But they are still in the minority and that
is why scientists are the very best allies of the idea of free speech and
academic freedom, because they still believe in evidence and in dis-
provability. For the rest of us in the university, in the social sciences and
humanities, the idea that there is no legitimate basis for privileging one
point of view over another holds a good deal of sway. Hence, there is an
absence of confidence within the university about the rules of argument
or methods of analysis or even in the nature and character of speech and
language. The absence of consensus about the means and objectives of
research and scholarship and their standards weakens the claim to free
speech because the ideal of a free forum for the unfettered exploration
of ideas from which a better or even the right answer or the truth will be
found, is no longer a shared goal of our contemporaries, one fully understood or subscribed to. The legitimate critique of some mythical rigid
positivist conceits that reigned before 1914 has run amok.

The third point is that the privileging of subjectivity has taken hold at
a time of radical displacement and anomie. Out there a powerful sense
of loneliness and isolation prevails. It is supplanted by and compensated by the solace of membership in groups. The ideal of the individual is
subordinated to membership in standardized notions of coherent communities. I escape the terror of individuality by becoming a member of
a group defined by sexual orientation, race or religion. Those groups may
be reductive in their definition but they function on a campus socially to
lessen the anxiety that the solitary experience of learning will in the end
translate into isolation. Going to campus in the American university can

be a lonely experience. That's why there are fraternities, and sororities, secret societies, and clubs. Students legitimately want to feel comfortable in a strange setting and they wish to be liked by their peers. The residential college and university is an unnatural situation. It boxes in people at the ages of 17 and 21 quite randomly into a single institution and expects civility. But there was never untarnished civility on the American campus. There was campus violence in the 18th and 19th century. The image that somehow once upon a time everybody was walking around as a kind of incipient scholar, who readily replaced violence for speech, is an historical myth. We are still more civilized than the Harvard and Yale of the first half of the 19th century, and we are probably ahead of the civility game in comparison to the age of the panty raids of the 1950s. The fact is that people are unsatisfied to be seen merely as individuals so they identify with groups and these groups happen now to generate their own sources of truth. Their perspective on the world is what seems to reign without question. And there is no appetite for criticism or empathy for dissent.

The subjective experience has deepened in this generation by the echo chamber provided by modern technology. Modern communication through social networks is virtual, as is friendship. Glued to their hand-held devices, individuals are passively engaging in a world that is actually imaginary, independent of space, materiality and real time and in which a technological illusion of intimacy, sharing and connection is fostered. There is no public space they must share with others—an agora, public square or even shopping mall to which all have access, which they have experienced, in which they meet others with whom their ideas and values might be contested. They connect online and form groups that are self-reinforcing. One does not emerge with the experience of how to defend a point of view against someone who differs but occupies the same neutral common ground, in real time and real space, on a train, on a plane, in a shop or town hall.

There is something ultimately cowardly about blogging, about putting notices on Facebook, and tweeting "likes." What I say to someone face to face requires a bit more courage even than writing it and sending an opinion into the vast digital space. I have colleagues who are very civilized in the presence of others and monstrous on e-mail. They emulate road rage; when they get behind the wheel, rigidity and resistance to empathy and compromise prevail. I can always apologize to someone in a conversation and retract: "let's forget what I said," "I regret it," or 'You misunderstood me, actually I didn't say that'. But the tweet and e-mail live forever, and they allow disputes never to be ultimately settled. When you post things, you cannot get rid of that post and you are going to apologize forever in vain. Technology undermines forgetting and forgiving, both indispensable acts in a civilized world. Technology allows the retrieval of the past beyond our natural memory and functions as a huge reinforcer of differences. This makes compromise and agreement very hard for the younger generation that has not actually experienced traditional public space. You walk down any campus and it is amazing how few people are talking to one another. They are texting or they are listening to devices. That novel isolation is compensated for by deep virtual allegiances to particular groups. That is the campus echo chamber.

My fourth point is that there is a growing moralizing intolerance with respect to any sort of deviancy. After all, a university, particularly its faculty, is a collection of deviants. There is no person who has been hired by a university of any quality who is not deviant by some demographic comparative measure. To be interested in classical languages, and to be interested in the fine points of poetry, quantum physics or any subject represented by the titles of articles or books published by university presses makes one by definition quite mad. To excel in the study of cell function or fossils and to be able to understand the questions of modern physics makes one an outlier. Yet administrative, governmental and legal pressures call for standardization and pressure for all to behave strictly to norms and to resist one's natural peculiarities and deviance. Faculty members are great as individuals because they are different, exceptional and resist being pigeonholed. And the university needs to protect them. But to control what exceptional individuals say, or how they behave, cuts against the qualities of deviance. One cannot segment the range and scope of exceptionalism. Nadia Boulanger or Marie Curie are unlikely to act in all ways in life just as your average person. Deviance that may be cognitive is probably linked, (though we do not know enough), to other forms of non-standard behavior. Eccentricity, even bizarre behavior is often aligned with talent and genius. Would Oscar Wilde succeed as a tenured professor? Those of us who are administrators at the university understand that part of our job is to protect the freedom of thought and speech of the odd individual who has certain gifts from the rage and envy of others. In my field, which is music, there are nothing but impossible but memorable and inspired personalities. It is a problem that the modern university now expects an increasing conformism in behavior as well as standardization of expressed thought. And that finally leads to a tremendous problem of self-censorship and passivity

Allison Stanger mentions in her section that the faculty and staff who signed up for the defense of academic freedom were by and large older. This suggests people with more of a historical memory of the period before the Vietnam War and World War II, or at least a consciousness of those events. They are themselves probably more frightened of the consequences of intolerance. It is absolutely true that what we face is a kind of new version of what used to be very doctrinal old left-wing and fascist views of liberal conceits about free speech, debate and argument and resistance to the notion of the free press. And let us not overlook the inherent conflict between commerce and the free press and the corruption that comes from needing to make a profit with the news—facts that damage the ideal of the role of the free press in democracy.

Nonetheless, we need to strengthen the belief that is still out there in the notion of truth, freedom and rational judgment and the links between democracy, liberty and social justice. The barriers to spreading those convictions include liberal inadequacies, liberal conceits and hypocrisy. The idea that freedom of speech and the life of the university are part of a complex burden in the way of realizing progress and social justice in an imperfect world, is hard to convey.

I had to debate a respected scholar this past year who believed that the whole enterprise of the university is a mirror image of an oppressive society which is designed to prevent those who are disadvantaged from reaching a status of dignity and equality. In that view, a conflict between the ideologies of free expression in research and learning and that of social justice dominates. There is some truth there. And this is not new. This claim was inherent in Soviet and state communist theory.

Now what is to be done about this? I have to say that my own view is that one has to have a sympathetic ear to why the younger generation, both faculty and students, don't see what we see. We need to break out of our own echo chamber and be quite clear that free expression and the habits of critique, skepticism and self-examination are absolutely indispensable. I happen to believe in that deeply, having an Eastern European Jewish background and being an immigrant. It seems second nature to me. I think scientists are of enormous and underutilized value in the leadership of universities in defending this. But I also think one has to hear very carefully that cloaked in the periodic craziness in which the American universities are now engaged, there is a severe reaction to a lot of undelivered claims in the American space. The disaffections go back to the election of Ronald Reagan. They concern claims about economic opportunity, about social justice, freedom, the right to vote, and about actually confronting racism. We are taking down statues of confederate generals but we are not erecting memorials for all the people who were lynched and killed after the Civil War. a huge hypocritical piety persists sometimes in the rhetoric of the defense of free speech; that hypocrisy is what Trump exploits. There are questions surrounding medical care, education or social services in the United States, all in a catastrophic situation. The university is viewed as in some way papering over or even tacitly defending inequities and injustices. We have to find a way to counter that claim and separate what we do and the idea of freedom of speech and academic freedom from any tacit alliance with those injustices.

We also need to defend the importance of language. One of the most terrifying things about the American campus now is the intent to identify what you stand for by the jargon you use. Hannah Arendt argued that real thinking starts when you find a way to use words differently. We need to resist identifying others using a reductive ideology marked by the use of certain vocabulary. It is the most noxious thing. a person in a university campus ought not be called to task for the use of vocabulary without any understanding of context, meaning or intent, let alone humor or irony. There is no way to make any kind of joke, even at the expense even of yourself. This is something that must be fought. But to fight it there must be more than generational moralizing.

We are in a situation that reminds me of the late 60s where the radicals of the 30s could not understand why the radicals of the 60s wouldn't listen to them. All they did was to moralize on the basis of "we were there" too. Pontification is not going to work when one seeks to sympathetically understand why young people with good hearts and with great potential have been so unbelievably bamboozled by misrepresentations, myths and the nonsensical. Take safe spaces. Critics ridicule the idea, even though the university in the past provided them—Cardinal Newman societies for Catholics and Hillel for Jews. Why object now to doing the same for others?

With empathy, there may be a way around the crisis, but finding that way takes a lot of patience. I am quite optimistic. But I think the university must be self-critical about the extent to which it cuts a path to defend what we need to defend; academic freedom and critical discourse cannot be compromised. We need to find the means to assemble allies on behalf of academic freedom and freedom of expression and realize a real commitment to address the issues of equity that seemed to have fallen off the agenda, even for the liberals since the Clinton era. This is why in some sense I think the election of Trump is a moment of dialectical opportunity; it has put an end to a certain complacency.

TAKING ACCOUNT OF ACADEMIC FREEDOM IN HUNGARY

Key Developments in Hungarian Higher Education
Attila Chikán

—— Attila Chikán is a Professor
Emeritus at Corvinus University,
Budapest and a Member of the CEU
Board of Trustees

The last quarter of a century was very turbulent in Hungarian higher education, even for a transition country. When Hungary faced transition at the end of the 1980s, there was a clear need for major changes in the Hungarian university system and in higher education in general. Hungary was ranked among the last ones on enrollment figures in Europe, due to the policies of the Communist regime. The quality of higher education was rather mixed. There were some very good universities, some high-level faculties, but also faculties and departments that were not as good as we wanted. My university, Corvinus, was very lucky, because at the end of the 1980s we had a program financed by George Soros, which made it possible for about 50 young professors to spend a year or at least a semester at the best American and Western European universities. This helped my university to get prepared for transition. It was a fundamental experience for our faculty, who gained personal and direct impressions of what university education is like in the most developed regions of the world.

On the organizational end, higher education was very unstable. There were a lot of discussions about the number and capacities of universities and higher education institutions. Hungary received funding from the World Bank to change the organizational structure, to have less institutions but higher overall capacity than we had at the time. The structural changes just started when the political transition introduced new turbulences. It is important to understand that the structural problems we are facing today are not new. Subsequent governments in Hungary after 1989 did not have a comprehensive policy for higher education. This led to constant instability. My university changed its faculty structure and its name four times in the past 25 years. This created an unfavorable environment for developing educational content. Financial resources were scarce and actually decreasing at universities. We were also very slow to respond to changes in the country; unfortunately higher education was not the driving force of intellectual change. Yet there was and there is gradual improvement in educational content. We have better courses, better educated teachers and better prepared and more talented students than 20 years ago. Even though we have a lot of problems with basic education, today's students are better prepared to meet the challenges posed by new developments of the global economy and global society.

Since the second Orbán government started to operate in 2010, there is a general tendency of centralization in higher education. In that sense, what is happening with universities is not very different from what is happening in other areas of life and institutional developments in Hungary. What is new is the appearance of political and ideological influence. When I was a department chair, member of the Senate and later Rector of Corvinus, I did experience much fewer attempts of political influence except through some financial pressures. Today we can observe striking examples of political influence, not only on the operational, but also in some cases at the academic level. This is very dangerous from the point of view of academic freedom.

In the early 90s, new laws were produced in all areas of life on a near-daily basis. The Parliament at that time worked like a machine, producing new laws which were tied to the ideas of market economy and the social developments we wanted to achieve. At the time, there was a heated debate whether we should follow a German or an Anglo-Saxon model in our higher education reforms. It was a meaningful debate and there were important arguments on both sides. In the end, we mixed the two, which was not very favorable, more or less inclined towards the Anglo-Saxon model. Fundamental questions were asked and answered in this process. There were not just minor changes in the curriculum or departmental reforms, but the whole philosophy of higher education and its role in society was at stake at the time. For example, the introduction of tuition fees was an important and interesting step. a number of professors (including myself), students and student organizations supported it as a step towards market economy and market-driven society. In our mind, it was supposed to go hand in hand with a system of scholarships and social support for students. Unfortunately, the government at the time picked up on the tuition fees issue and abolished it.

Legal changes in Hungarian Higher education: 1993-1999

Higher education law [Law LXXX]

1993	<ul><li>Warranting institutional autonomy.</li><li>Universities are run by a Senate and the Rector, little external intervention allowed.</li><li>Establishes a system of doctoral schools similar to Western European and the US</li><li>Founding new universities by the Catholic and Reformed Church</li><li>Efforts of making the Hungarian higher education compatible with international standards, including the acceptance of Hungarian diplomas abroad.</li></ul>

Legal changes in Hungarian Higher education: 1993-1999	
1995	**Introduction of tuition fees** • Abolished after a referendum in 1998
1999	**Amendment of the Higher education law [Law LII]** • Merges various institutions and reduces their number to 62 • Centralizes the nomination of university professors to a state accreditation institution • Still allows extensive autonomy

Figure 1. Own compilation

There was almost permanent legal change, and from 2010 onwards, a new wave of centralization hit. The independence of universities was hurt in many ways. One of them was the introduction of the chancellor system, which is rather different from the chancellor system in US universities. True, the organization and financing of universities was not in order, there had to be changes. But the reform centralized a lot of the management of universities and distributed power between the rector and the chancellor in a way that impacted the freedom of universities negatively. Of course, there are differences between chancellors of universities. In some places the system operates adequately, in other places not. But the idea itself was steered towards centralization. The 2017 change to the higher education law came as a surprise. Even though we had constant change with a tendency towards centralization, this one was a step towards politics-oriented instead of academics-oriented decisionmaking. It didn't follow from the previous developments.

	Legal changes in Hungarian Higher education: 2005-2017
2005	**New Higher education law [Law CXXXIX]** • Centralization of admissions and adoption of the Bologna system, • Introduction of Economic Councils in the universities, supervising the economic management of the universities
2011	**New Higher education law [Law CCIV]** • Rectors nominated by the Minister and not the Senate • Minister can centrally allocate the scholarships and tuition waivers available
2013	**Constitutional amendment** • Restricting university autonomy in the basic law
2014	**Amendments to the Higher education law** • Introduces centrally nominated Chancellors, deciding all financial and administrative issues • Indirectly they can influence the hiring of teachers
2017	**Amendment to the Higher Education law "Lex CEU"**

Figure 2. Own compilation

I would like to finish with some illustrations tot show that the current higher education policy is neither efficient nor favorable. The number of students is declining. Of course the population is declining too, but at a much smaller rate.

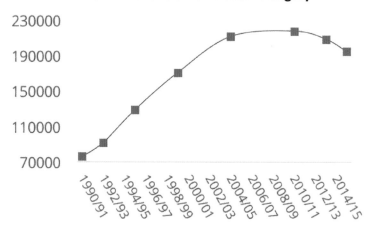

Overall student enrollment in Hungary

Figure 3. Source: Péter Radó, "A felsőoktatás állami megszállásáról és annak következményeiről," *Beszélő,* May 22, 2015, http://beszelo.c3.hu/onlinecikk/a-felsooktatas-allami-megszallasarol-es-annak-kovetkezmenyeirol.

It is even worse that higher education spending has been going down in the last few years. Though it slightly increased in 2015 and 2016 it is still far from the peak we started from.

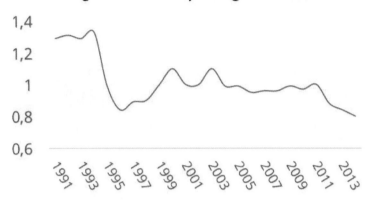

Higher education spending in % of GDP

Figure 4. Source: Own compilation based on the yearbooks of the Ministry of Education / Ministry of Human Resources

What is also striking is that in terms public expenditure on tertiary education, Hungary ranks at the end of the OECD measure, only Italy spending less as a percentage of its GDP.

Public Expenditure on tertiary education as % of public spending 2013

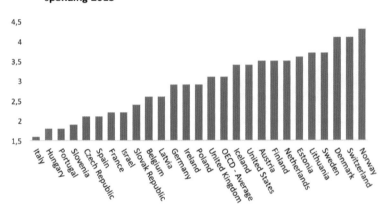

Figure 5, Source: Source: OECD, Education at a Glance 2016: OECD Indicators, OECD Publishing, 2016, doi:10.1787/eag-2016-en.

I think it is important to note that people are unhappy with the way higher education and education in general is developing in Hungary. There were several demonstrations by university students and high school teachers for academic freedom and for better education in general. I think it is important to understand that those people who are most affected by the changes, those young people who face the higher education system today, would like to see a different way ahead.

The problems of Hungarian higher education are very deeply rooted in their social and political background. Transition created in principle an opportunity to change some of the trends which we have experienced. But instead of that, the political intentions of the 1990s and 2000s have generally overruled academic considerations. Because of that, higher education as such could not move into the direction which both its own and global requirements demanded. After the hectic developments described above, there were many expectations concerning the higher education policy of the Orbán government. It is disappointing that the government did not move closer towards the demands of education in the 21st century. Many rules and laws are in fact pointing towards the opposite direction. One of the most significant parts is the attack against CEU, which is a flagship of academic quality and freedom in Hungary. I think this is not what Hungarian society requires, and it is not what Hungary needs to get into a better position in an increasingly complex and globalized world. There is a need for a fundamental change of direction.

University Autonomy in Hungary in Perspective
István Kenesei

—— *István Kenesei is a Professor Emeritus of Linguistics at the University of Szeged.*

As Professor Scott argued so eloquently in her introductory talk, university autonomy is the prerequisite to academic freedom. Academic freedom on the other hand is the prerequisite for critical thinking. And from Karl Popper's *The Logic of Scientific Discovery* I have learnt that critical thinking is the bedrock of university-level education.[1]

To draw some light on the state of university autonomy in Hungary, I would like to present some striking insights from the latest European University Association survey, based on data from 2015 and 2016.[2] It mentions four dimensions and several related properties that are commonly used to define university autonomy:

[1] Karl Popper, *The Logic of Scientific Discovery* (London: Hutchinson, 1972).
[2] Enora Benetot Pruvot and Thomas Estermann, "University Autonomy in Europe III: The Scorecard 2017," 2017, http://www.eua.be/Libraries/publications/University-Autonomy-in-Europe-2017.

The European University Association's 4 dimensions of university autonomy in Europe	
Organizational Autonomy	A university's ability to decide freely on its internal organization and executive head.
Financial Autonomy	A university's ability to decide freely on its internal financial affairs.
Staffing Autonomy	A university's ability to decide freely on issues related to human resources management, including recruitments, salaries, dismissals and promotions.
Academic Autonomy	A university's ability to decide on various academic issues, such as student admissions, academic content, quality assurance, the introduction of degree programs and the language of instruction.

Figure 1[3]

If we look at the development in Hungary's ranking in the survey, we can see that it has declined on most principles. In terms of organizational autonomy, it has fallen from number 16 in 2011 to 23 in 2017. In terms of financial autonomy, it has dropped from 6 all the way to 23 and in staffing autonomy from 17 to 22. Hungary has only improved in terms academic autonomy, from 24 to 16. It is important to note though that as for this last property, the option to select quality assurance boards counts for 26% of the overall score. Thus, Hungary has boosted its standing by the single act of allowing Hungarian universities this freedom of choice.

[3] Ibid.

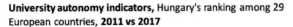

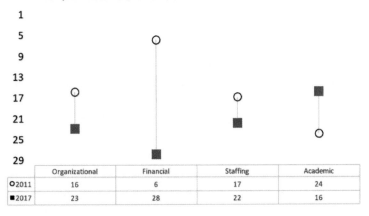

Figure 2. Source: European University Association

The merging and splitting up of institutions are done by decree, usually without consulting them. Two recent examples: Faculties from other
universities have been moved into the new University of Public Administration and another institution favored by the government, the University
of Physical Education, was split off from Semmelweis University. Rectors'
elections were overruled in 2013 at two universities, where the top selected candidates were not nominated by the Ministry, which had never
happened before. There was an uproar, even in the Hungarian Rectors'
Conference, so the government retraced its steps, but as a countermea-
sure it has subsequently imposed chancellors as heads of university
finances and administration. a chancellor is selected by the Ministry and
appointed by the Prime Minister without the Senate or the Rector having
a say in it. Chancellors are not only hired and employed by the Minister
but they are regularly invited to conferences in the Ministry, where they
get their instructions. They have full power in hiring non-academics and

in any financial decision. All in all, they are a foreign body to a university. There used to be finance managers at universities, who could object on rational or legal grounds to the Rector's or the Senate's decisions on financial matters, which was not problematic because the finance manager was integral to the university and not subservient to a ministry.

Budget-wise, there has been a long process of change since 1993, when the first law on higher education was enacted by the first freely elected, and truly conservative, government in Hungary. The liberal legislation that they introduced and which provided for clear budgetary norms doesn't exist anymore. Government-funded students are allocated to various degree programs and various universities again by decree. The rest of the budgets are decided on a case-by-case basis by the Ministry, with the privileged institutions getting extra subsidies. EU funding, amounting to several billion forints' worth, is allocated to various universities without applying any general principles.

Independence of the Hungarian Accreditation Committee has also been a serious issue. In 1993, half of the members were selected by the Academy of Sciences, and half of them by universities and various other organizations. Now, half of the members are appointed by the Minister and the other half by various other organizations, including the Rectors' Conference or various bodies favored by the government, such as the new Arts Academy or the Chamber of Commerce.[4] In the 1993 law of higher education it was enacted that funding for the Accreditation Committee was decided by Parliament, which is no longer the case. Moreover, the Minister must now give prior consent to any new degree program submitted to the Accreditation Committee. The Ministry can thus preempt, but also effec-

---

[4] See: "1993 Hungarian Higher Education Act (1993. évi LXXX. Törvény a Felsőoktatásról)" (1993), https://mkogy.jogtar.hu/?page=show&docid=99300080.TV. and "2011 Hungarian National Act on Higher Education (2011. évi CCIV. Törvény a Nemzeti Felsőoktatásról)" (2011), http://net.jogtar.hu/jr/gen/hjegy_doc.cgi?docid=A1100204.TV&celpara=#xcelparam.

tively overrule the Committee's decision. Furthermore, degree programs can be abruptly terminated by the Ministry, and certain degree programs are only assigned to selected universities. For example, public administration can only be taught at the University of Public Administration.

What lessons can be learnt from all this? Lamentably, there has been little resistance by academics or by rectors. To illustrate how far we have progressed downhill, the Secretary for Education has recently sent a letter to one of our universities declaring that the maximum salaries of professors, whether or not they have their extra bonuses from EU projects, cannot exceed that of a section head in the Ministry. Or one can mention the Rectors' Conference's inept objection over Lex CEU, complaining only for their universities possibly not receiving sufficient numbers of foreign students in consequence. On the other hand, there have been mass demonstrations in support of CEU, rallying students and academics in and outside Hungary. Therefore, I think that there is still hope that we will be able to stand up against the repression of university autonomy and academic freedom.

Historical Foundations of Academic Freedom in Hungary —— *Katalin Tausz*

—— *Katalin Tausz is a Professor at the Department of Social Policy at ELTE University, Budapest*

I would like to raise a fundamental question:
What is the purpose of a university?

The founding of the university of Nagyszombat, Péter Pázmány in the middle (source: https://ppke.hu/)

Take my own university, Eötvös Loránd (ELTE). It was founded in 1635 in the small rural town of Nagyszombat, today Trnava in Slovakia, by Cardinal Péter Pázmány as a Catholic university for teaching theology and philosophy. According to the founding deed of the university, "It was of utmost importance for the university to temper the nature of a pugnacious nation, and to educate people capable to govern the church and to serve the state." Let me emphasize this: to serve the state.

Portray of József Eötvös by Gyula Stetka (source: Wikimedia Commons)

There is another leading figure in the history of education in Hungary, József Eötvös. He happens to be the father of Loránd Eötvös, who wrote in his famous work Influence of the Ruling Ideas of the 19th century on the State that literacy or education is a precondition of liberty and freedom. József Eötvös wrote that the university should be based on the equality of faculties, freedom of research of the professors and the liberty to present scientific results and conviction. To Eötvös, knowledge is the precondition of freedom. From that it follows that the objective of the university must be to develop free individuals for a free society. The precondition for this is good education. Though Eötvös described his vision for the university in detail, it was never fully realized.

Portray of Wilhelm von Humboldt by Franz Krüger (source: Wikimedia Commons)

After the revolution in the 19th century it was not József Eötvös' ideas which were at the heart of the new university system in Hungary but, as in many other European countries, the ideas of Wilhelm von Humboldt. According to Humboldt, science is the free activity of human beings. Freedom is the dominant principle of science and the university. The role of the university is not to provide civil servants and good Christian subjects for the state, but to teach and exercise science in the spirit of academic freedom. Humboldt argued that students should have the right to choose their professors. Thus, the council of the university and the state should not have direct control over education so that the university is strengthened through real autonomy

Let's put these ideas together. Cardinal Péter Pázmány wanted to educate people to serve the state. József Eötvös said that education and literacy are the preconditions of freedom and a free society. Then Humboldt said that the purpose of the university is not to create good subjects for the state, but knowledgeable, critical thinking and autonomous individuals. These ideas were enshrined in Hungary's previous constitution, which was in effect until 2010. It said: "The Republic of Hungary shall respect and support the freedom of scientific and artistic expression, the freedom to learn and to teach. Only scientists are entitled to decide on questions of scientific truth and to determine the scientific value of research." In 2010, the constitution was replaced by the new Fundamental Law of Hungary. It says: "Hungary shall protect the scientific and artistic freedom of the Hungarian Academy of Sciences and the Hungarian Academy of Arts." The difference is obvious. We went from the protection of the freedom of scientific and artistic expression to the scientific and artistic freedom of the Academy of Sciences, which is financed by the government. This is reflected in the figures presented by István Kenesei, where Hungary has declined on nearly all measures of university autonomy in Europe. This raises a number of daunting questions on the state of academic freedom in today's Hungary. Most of all, whether today's legal and institutional system is in line with the fundamental ideas of Eötvös and Humboldt or those of Pázmány.

Academic Freedom and Quality Assurance
in Hungarian Universities ——— *Valéria Csépe*

*——— Valéria Csépe is President of
the Hungarian Higher Education
Accreditation Committee (HAC)*

In September 2016, I became president of the Hungarian Higher Education Accreditation Committee (HAC). Since then, different decisions were
made to change the working style of HAC and to abandon its previous
role; HAC has often been seen as the policeman of higher education institutions in Hungary. In the past years, HAC has been operating as a critical
partner with its stakeholders when changes or reforms were introduced,
including legislative changes in higher education. This had a considerable
impact on the question of how the autonomy of higher education institutions should be changed in terms of increasing the universities' responsibility towards quality assurance.

When we take the point of view of an accreditation committee, data by
the European University Association indicates that Hungary belongs to
the countries where universities can choose a quality assurance agency
freely and according to their needs. This includes agencies from other
EU countries. From this point of view, Hungary has a relatively high score
and seems to be doing well. The Primary Law states: "Higher education
institutions shall be autonomous in terms of content and the methods

of research and teaching, their organization shall be regulated by an act. The government shall, within the framework of an act, lay down the rules governing the financial management of public higher education institutions and shall supervise their financial management." In themselves, these are robust constitutional provisions. However, the question is how all these work in practice. If we look at the University Autonomy Scorecard published by the European University Association, we see that Hungary ranks very low on nearly all indicators. Its poor performance is rooted in a restrictive legislative process which is based on a paternalistic view of higher education that has historic roots in Hungary. For a long time, there has been the assumption that policymakers and politicians know better than academics how to run a university. This attitude is in contradiction with the integrity and autonomy of higher education institutions and in general with academic freedom.

Further questions arise when higher education quality assurance criteria are considered. What are the students' interests at our universities and how well do we evaluate the outcomes of higher education? From this point of view, there are further sources of violation. Here we may see how some stakeholders such as professors in different positions and committees violate the academic freedom of others; when judging on new courses, new programs, new doctoral schools. Often this is rooted only in counterproductive competition; in Hungary we have learned to compete but not to cooperate. This is very important as there is a considerable imbalance between competition and cooperation. On the other hand, professional judgement of academics may be influenced by political bias as well. This is very difficult to trace and to correct. Still, it is highly important to prevent this, particularly via inviting foreign experts to the accreditation process.

There are also different kinds of unconscious bias. Therefore, we must prevent any negative effect, be it as a result of intolerance or orthodoxy. People in high-ranking positions may be intolerant towards new programs or to free inquiry. Decades ago in my own profession I experienced how intolerant mainstream psychology can be towards new areas such as cognitive science and neuroscience. Now research and higher education in these fields are internationally recognized. Two of my former colleagues working at CEU are among the most cited researchers of theoretical and cognitive neuroscience. Their contribution to the performance of Hungarian higher education is significant as they produce outstanding results; quality and excellence is what counts.

A further problem that is important to mention, to know and prevent from a quality assurance point of view is the small country effect, seen in all types of evaluation. In the US, the job market has a fantastic regulatory role that steers the universities' responsibility for quality assurance. There, you know what a PhD as a degree means when it comes from Harvard or MIT as compared to a less recognized university. That, we do not have here yet and it is one of the many barriers we face and need to change if we want to have progress in academic quality and at the end in academic freedom. We have to do a lot to improve our practices. We have a long way to go.

The Situation in Hungary from the Perspective of Private Universities —— *László Vass*

—— *László Vass is President of the Private Institutions Section at the Hungarian Rectors' Conference and Rector of Budapest Metropolitan University*

Hungary is very bureaucratic in some ways. Governments love to regulate, no matter if it is necessary or not. This is centuries' long history, it is not new, but for private universities it can be uncomfortable. We have to comply with most higher education regulations with one small exception, the employment of teachers. In the public sector, teachers are public employees. We, private universities, on the other hand operate under the general labor code, which governs the private and business sector. Our teachers generally do not have such stable and protected positions as the ones in public universities. Yet it gives us more flexibility in many respects.

The big question we are asking here is what is the role of academic freedom and autonomy in the 21st century, particularly, what is the mission of a private higher education institution? I love that vision of Humboldt and the 19th century unified utopia about the elite academic cast having high social respect and special privileges in society. But is this vision still appropriate today? We, the private universities and colleges in Hungary, feel that the capitalist market economy has destroyed such protected enclaves in our society. Why should professors enjoy a protected position?

Because they have the knowledge, others do not. The biggest tensions are between politicians and professors. a politician was born to know everything, the professors learned everything. That is a problem.

If we want to understand our current problems, we need to examine closer also the history of public administration in Hungary, which has been centralized and step-by-step politicized over the past 27 years. Every successive government moved a step closer towards a *spoils system* of public administration. This has been happening in the field of higher education too. Yet I do not see much direct pressure or intervention from the government against academic freedom. The reality is more subtle. There are various traditional patterns of obedience, often political expectations are assumed rather than directly communicated or enforced.

Over hundreds of years in history, Hungarians learned to cope. On one hand you obey, on the other hand you cheat the government. Because relations and regulations are often not very transparent and complete, people know very well how to behave. The government wants to do this, we do that. This tradition is obviously not acceptable. We need clear normative regulations which are transparent and under which we can operate well. We obviously need more autonomy, but also more efficient and effective regulation. When we started our private university, we realized within two years that we can do everything at 20 percent lower costs than a state university, because we operate much more efficiently. We got a chancellor as demanded by our owners, whom we call our executive director. This position is highly ranked, it helped us to ensure our operations in the most economical way, and to use our resources much better.

In a very fragmented higher education system, the government always has a headache about finance. We see in the figures that István Kenesei presents how unstable the level of higher education finance has been.

Unfortunately, we are a four-year country. We have parliamentary elections every four years. Everything starts again after the election of a new government, but higher education policy should be much longer-term. It does not work on a four-year policy cycle. Eight years of stability may be regarded as the minimum, but we have not had more than four years of stability at a time over the past 25 years, this is a big problem.

Finally, I want to raise what I believe are the key questions ahead: What is the vision of higher education in the 21st century? What is the mission of universities? What is the position of highly-educated researchers and professors in society? What does autonomy mean in a globalized and networked world? We are all financially, scientifically and social networked and we depend on those networks.

Freedom and Its Enemies, or How To Be a Good Citizen in a Tangled World —— *Mario Vargas Llosa*

—— *Mario Vargas Llosa is a Peruvian writer and scholar and the 2010 Nobel Laureate for literature.*

> Freedom is a valuable good, but no country and no human being can ever be sure of it, if he is not able to own it, to exercise it and to defend it. Literature, which breathes because of it and suffocates without it, can make you comprehend that freedom is not a gift of the heavens but a choice, a conviction, a practice and a set of beliefs that need to be constantly enriched and tested. (Excerpt from Vargas Llosa's acceptance speech of the Peace Prize of the German Book Trade, 1996 [translated])[1]

When the students at CEU finish their studies, they must be prepared to enter a world which is difficult, with plenty of opportunities but also with many uncertainties; a world transformed by the extraordinary technical revolutions of the last years, but also a world in which jobs that were taken for granted for everybody are becoming more and more a privilege, a world in which, when you want to have a job, you have to invent it and create it yourself. I am sure that graduates of CEU are well trained to face

---

[1] Mario Vargas Llosa, "Dank: Dinosaurier in Schweren Zeiten," 1996, http://www.frie-denspreis-des-deutschen-buchhandels.de/sixcms/media.php/1290/1996_Llosa.pdf.

the challenges of this new world. CEU prepares students to be good professionals but also to be good citizens which I think is one of the obligations of any serious academic institution in the world in which we live.

What does it mean to be a good citizen? It does not only mean to be a law-abiding citizen, cultivated and alert, with a culture that does not allow oneself to be manipulated by the powers of this world. I think the essential feature of a good citizen is that he or she has a critical spirit. Such citizens do not permit themselves to be convinced by the powers that be that they are living in the best of worlds. No society is the best of all worlds. There is always something lacking and it is indispensable to believe there could be better opportunities and a better life. This is something that only democracy permits.

We are very lucky that the worst enemies of democratic culture and of democratic society—racism, fascism, and communism—have been defeated in our times. The Soviet Union has collapsed because of its inability to satisfy the most elementary ambitions of its population. China has become a capitalist country. It is still a dictatorship, but a capitalist dictatorship. I don't think there are many rational, sensible people who would think that countries like Cuba or Venezuela are a model, if you want to have a free, well-adjusted country. Democracy now has the world to itself and is making progress. When I was young in Latin America we had dictatorships from one extreme to the other with only three exceptions: Chile, Costa Rica and Uruguay. Now what we have, with the exception of Cuba and Venezuela, are democracies which are imperfect even highly corrupt, but a bad democracy is much better than a good dictatorship.

> All our efforts will be directed toward turning Peru from the country of proletarians, the unemployed, and the privi-

leged elites that it is today into a country of entrepreneurs, property owners, and citizens equal before the law. (Mario Vargas Llosa, *A Fish in the Water*)[2]

The enemies of democracy are now within democracies themselves: populism and nationalism. They are not the same thing. Populism is more than nationalism, but an essential aspect of populism is nationalism. Both are reactions to globalization. Globalization is a reality, but not everybody is happy. Many people are afraid about the opening of borders. They are terrified and they are succumbing to what Karl Popper called the temptation of the tribe: to regress to a primitive state where everybody knows everybody, where you can be assured because everyone speaks your language, shares your beliefs and customs.

> Totalitarianism is not simply amoral. It is the morality of the closed society—of the group, or of the tribe; it is not individual selfishness, but it is collective selfishness. (*Karl Popper*)[3]

This kind of tribal temptation is still present in many countries. I think this is what is behind the conspiracy to close the Central European University. The government does not like what this institution is doing: training students to be good professionals, but also to be good citizens, democratic citizens with an alert and critical spirit. They thought it would be easy to close this institution, a discrete operation. They made a law to justify their act but were extremely surprised because it turned out to be not as discrete and secret as they would have liked it to be. Because there was a reaction, a strong reaction, not only in Hungary, not only in Europe but also in the US and in other countries all over the world.

---

[2] Mario Vargas Llosa, *A Fish in the Water: A Memoir* (New York: Picador, 1993), 181.
[3] Karl Popper, *Open Society and Its Enemies* (London: Routledge, 2011), 108.

What has happened is extremely important. Thousands of people all over the world have understood that what is happening here is a battle for the future of Europe, for the Europe we are constructing now.

> In a world of permanent change we cannot, according to [Karl] Popper, 'return to the alleged innocence and beauty of the closed society', without sparking the destructive force, which has already been forgotten in Europe. In Latin America you can see where this leads to. (Mario Vargas Llosa in an interview with the *Neue Züricher Zeitung* in 2016)[4]

The Europe that we are building is probably the most ambitious project of a culture of freedom in history. It is a reality and has produced almost seventy years of peace on a continent which has been destroying itself for a long time. We now have a construction that represents something extremely ambitious, not only for Europe but also for the rest of the world.

True, many things can be criticized about the construction of Europe. There is too much bureaucratization. Brussels does not reach the base of society. One of the problems with the construction of Europe is that only political and cultural elites are aware of its global importance. Many Europeans have not embraced the enthusiasm that is necessary for the idea of Europe. But they receive the benefits. When I went to Spain for the first time as a young student it was an underdeveloped country with a brutal dictatorship, totally isolated from the rest of the world. In Lima, in the diversity of San Marco University, we knew more about what was going on in France and in Italy than in Madrid. Look at Spain now! It has moved from dictatorship to democracy, from an underdeveloped to a developed

---

[4] Michael Wiederstein, "Literatur Ist Rebellion," *Neue Züricher Zeitung*, July 7, 2016, https://www.nzz.ch/feuilleton/mario-vargas-llosa-im-gespraech-literatur-ist-rebellion-ld.104313.

country. The middle class has grown enormously and it is a democratic country. This would not have been possible without Europe. If you examine the countries of Europe you will see how the EU has helped each to profit. When you balance out what has been achieved against the problems that exist in Europe, the present seems enormously favorable. Therefore, I am quite optimistic for the future. But we need to further try to reach the base of society in Europe through different means.

The defense of CEU is a defense of what Europe wants to be, the creation of a culture of freedom. It is this culture that has produced the most important social, cultural and political achievements in the history of mankind. Within Europe we have enemies of democracy, people who are terrified by the opening of borders, by coexistence in diversity, in cultural, social and political terms. They want to regress in history to the old times, the times of closed nationalities, the times of the tribes.

I belief that many prejudices that were raised against globalization are unfounded. The idea that globalization is going to standardize the world and that not only languages but also customs and beliefs are going to be made uniform is completely absurd. French culture will not disappear with globalization, neither will English or Spanish culture. To the contrary, in this open space, cultures will have the possibility not only to develop but to enrich themselves through this coexistence. Globalization erodes borders which after religions have been the major source of wars, brutality and violence in the history of humankind. It is not destroying the nation. It is pacifying what is potentially violent in the idea of the nation. Nations are not disappearing but they are changing dramatically. Europe was full of hate until very recently. The best demonstration of this are the two world wars in which millions of Europeans disappeared. If there is a continent in which globalization should be received with open arms, it is Europe.

You may tell me now that contrary to my ideas one must always be a citizen of a given country, you can't be a citizen of everywhere. Then I would reply: But why not? You can be a citizen of Europe. Many Europeans have different nationalities because of the arbitrariness of history. I still believe in the attachment to a country which is for example an attachment to a language. You feel that your language is something essential to you. My attachment to Spanish makes me attached to Peru, to Colombia and at least twenty-three countries in the world. Customs were much more uniform in the past. Now you have the possibility to be different, a kind of opportunity that we did not have before. If you were French you were French, and if not, you were a traitor. Now you can choose. If you feel better in a certain country than yours, you have not only the opportunity but also the right to become Hungarian, Russian or even Chinese. These are freedoms that we did not have in the past and I think we should celebrate them.

I do not think that this conspiracy against academic freedom, against the culture of freedom and against democracy is going to prevail. The reaction has been enormous. Academics, writers, teachers and politicians have been mobilized, feeling that if this conspiracy succeeds in Hungary, the European project is under threat. It may happen again in other countries and the minority which is still resisting this opening of the borders and this integration in diversity that Europe represents will also be threatened. Freedom is not divisible, you cannot fragment it and use only one aspect of freedom and reject the others. If you have economic freedom but no political freedom, economic freedom does not work. If you have political freedom but no economic freedom, it does not work either. Freedom is indivisible, you have to accept it with all the risks that without a doubt come with it. Freedom brings enormous challenges, but when you accept it, you know that you will not only have risks but also extraordinary achievements: peace, the security to live in a legal structure which protects you against the arbitrariness of the powers of this world and also diversity of beliefs, of convictions, of ideas that permits a democratic society to learn from its mistakes. Democracy is indeed the only system that learns from its mistakes.

Books and writers can play an enormous role in upholding a culture of freedom. All dictatorships in history, all authoritarian regimes that wanted to control life from beginning to end have been suspicious of literature and created systems of censorship and control. We are only surprised in democracy that books can be dangerous. But dictators know better than us. In a dictatorship books always threaten power. Why? Because books become a way through which people become informed of what TV, radio and newspapers don't cover. When Hungary was a satellite of the Soviet Union, Hungarians read books to figure out what was going on. They immediately went to literature to have the kind of information that reality did not provide. This is dangerous, because after you read a good novel and when you return to the real world, what you discover is that the worlds that we writers invent are much better than the real world. You discover in yourself a malaise when facing the real world and you become unsatisfied. Dissatisfaction is very dangerous for regimes that want to demonstrate that reality is perfect. That is the reason why dictatorships are very suspicious of literature. Literature is very important to awaken the critical spirit which is essential in democratic society.

There are so many writers in Europe who are trying to save CEU from this conspiracy against freedom. They are also trying to save the culture of freedom and the future Europe we want. If we win I think there are great chances that we will also win the war against populism, nationalism and all the enemies of the culture of freedom. But what if we fail? Believe me, we will not fail. We have no reason to be pessimistic.

References

1993 Hungarian Higher Education Act (1993. évi LXXX. törvény a felsőoktatásról) (1993). https://mkogy.jogtar. hu/?page=show&docid=99300080.TV.

2011 Hungarian National Act on Higher Education (2011. évi CCIV. törvény a nemzeti felsőoktatásról) (2011). http://net.jogtar.hu/jr/gen/hjegy_doc.cgi?docid=A1100204.TV&celpara=#xcelparam.

AAUP. "Declaration of Principles on Academic Freedom and Tenure," 1915.

Abrami, Regina. M., William C. Kirby, and F. Warren McFarlan. "Why China Can't Innovate." *Harvard Business Review*, no. March 2014 (2014).

Agerholm, Harriet. "Harvard, Yale and Stanford Sue Donald Trump over His 'Muslim Travel Ban.'" *The Independent*, February 14, 2017. http://www.independent.co.uk/news/world/americas/harvard-yale-stanford-suing-donald-trump-muslim-ban-lawsuit-us-immigration-restriction-a7579886.html.

Ali, Aftab. "Oxford University Students Call for Greater 'Racial Sensitivity' at the Institution and Say It Must Be 'Decolonised' | The Independent." *Independent*, 2015. http://www.independent.co.uk/student/news/oxford-university-students-call-for-greater-racial-sensitivity-at-the-institution-and-say-it-must-be-10332118.html.

APSA. "Statement on Violence at Middlebury College on March 2," 2017. http://www.apsanet.org/Portals/54/goverance/2017/

APSA Statement on Violence at Middlebury College on March 2.pdf?ver=2017-03-09-102506-453.

Ash, Timothy Garton. "To Fight the Xenophobic Populists, We Need More Free Speech, Not Less." *The Guardian*, May 12, 2011. https://www.theguardian.com/commentisfree/2011/may/12/fight-xenophobic-populists-need-free-speech.

Baer, Ulrich. "What 'Snowflakes' Get Right About Free Speech." *The New York Times*, April 24, 2017. https://www.nytimes.com/2017/04/24/opinion/what-liberal-snowflakes-get-right-about-free-speech.html.

Bromwich, David. "Academic Freedom and Its Opponents." In *Who`s Affraid of Academic Freedom?*, edited by Akeel Bilgrami and Jonathan R. Cole, 27–40. New York: Columbia University Press, 2015.

Chorley, Lord. "Academic Freedom in the United Kingdom." *Law and Contemporary Problems* 28, no. 3 (January 1963): 647. http://www.jstor.org/stable/1190651?origin=crossref.

Cole, Jonathan R. "Academic Freedom under Fire." In *Who`s Affraid of Academic Freedom?*, edited by Akeel Bilgrami and Jonathan R. Cole, 40–67. New York: Columbia University Press, 2015.

———. *Toward a More Perfect University*. Public Affairs, 2016.

Elgayar, Aisha. "Arab Students Caught in Regional Conflict With Qatar." *Al-Fanar Media*, June 13, 2017. https://www.al-fanarmedia.org/2017/06/arab-students-caught-regional-conflict-qatar/.

Free Inquiry on Campus. "Free Inquiry on Campus: A Statement of Principles by over One Hundred Middlebury College Professors," 2017. https://freeinquiryblog.wordpress.com/.

Friedersdorf, Conor. "The Campus-Speech Debate Spends Summer Break in Statehouses." *The Atlantic*, September 3, 2017. https://www.

theatlantic.com/politics/archive/2017/08/the-campus-speech-debate-is-summering-in-statehouses/535608/.

Goldstein, Dana. "After Charlottesville Violence, Colleges Brace for More Clashes." *New York Times*, August 16, 2017. https://www.nytimes.com/2017/08/16/us/after-charlottesville-violence-colleges-brace-for-more-clashes.html.

Havel, Vaclav. "The Power of the Powerless." *Http://www.vaclavhavel.cz*, 1978. http://www.vaclavhavel.cz/showtrans.php?cat=eseje&val=2_aj_eseje.html&typ=HTML.

Herfurth, Theodore. "Sifting and Winnowing: A Chapter in the History of Academic Freedom at the University of Wisconsin," 1949.

Kadıoğlu, Ayşe. *Cumhuriyet İradesi, Demokrasi Muhakemesi : Türkiye'de Demokratik Açılım Arayışları*. Metis Yayınları, 1999. http://www.metiskitap.com/catalog/book/4315.

Kant, Immanuel. *The Conflict of the Faculties (Der Streit Der Fakultäten)*. Edited by Mary J Gregor. Lincoln: University of Nebraska Press, 1979.

King Abdullah University of Science and Technology. "Faculty Handbook," 2015. https://academicaffairs.kaust.edu.sa/faculty-affairs/Documents/Faculty Handbook 2015-16 (updated 22 Mar 2016).pdf.

Kipnis, Laura. "Sexual Paranoia Strikes Academe." *The Chronicle of Higher Education*, February 27, 2015. http://www.chronicle.com/article/Sexual-Paranoia-Strikes/190351.

Llosa, Mario Vargas. *A Fish in the Water: A Memoir*. New York: Picador, 1993.

———. "Dank: Dinosaurier in Schweren Zeiten," 1996. http://www.friedenspreis-des-deutschen- buchhandels.de/sixcms/media.php/1290/1996_Llosa.pdf.

Matei, Liviu, and Julia Iwinska. "University Autonomy: A Practical Handbook." Budapest, 2014.

Minow, Martha, and Robert Post. "Standing up for 'so-Called' Law." *Boston Globe*, February 10, 2017. https://www.bostonglobe.com/opinion/2017/02/10/standing-for-called-law/VLbDYmrwpdjCn8qs5FPJaK/story.html.

Miyoshi, M. "Ivory Tower in Escrow." *Boundary 2* 27, no. 1 (March 1, 2000): 7–50. doi:10.1215/01903659-27-1-7.

"My Title IX Inquisition." *The Chronicle of Higher Education*, May 29, 2015. http://www.chronicle.com/article/My-Title-IX-Inquisition/230489.

Newfield, Christopher. *Unmaking the Public University: The Forty Year Assault on the Middle Class*. Cambridge: Harvard University Press, 2011.

OECD. *Education at a Glance 2016: OECD Indicators*. OECD Publishing, 2016. doi:10.1787/eag-2016-en.

Office of the Provost. "Zayed University Faculty Handbook," 2009. http://www.zu.ac.ae/main/files/contents/edu/docs/accr/faculty_handbook.pdf.

Özkirimli, Umut. "How to Liquidate a People? Academic Freedom in Turkey and Beyond." *Globalizations*, May 22, 2017, 1–6. doi:10.1080/14747731.2017.1325171.

Parini, Jay, and Keegan Callanan. "Middlebury's Statement of Principle." *The Wall Street Journal*, March 6, 2017. https://www.wsj.com/articles/middleburys-statement-of-principle-1488846993.

Patton, Laurie L. "The Right Way to Protect Free Speech on Campus - WSJ." *The Wall Street Jounral*, June 6, 2017. https://www.wsj.com/articles/the-right-way-to-protect-free-speech-on-campus-1497019583.

Popper, Karl. *The Logic of Scientific Discovery*. London: Hutchinson, 1972.

———. *Open Society and Its Enemies*. London: Routledge, 2011.

Post, Robert. *The Classic First Amendment Tradition Under Stress: Freedom of Speech and the University*. [unpublished], 2017.

Pruvot, Enora Benetot, and Thomas Estermann. "University Autonomy in Europe III: The Scorecard 2017," 2017. http://www.eua.be/Libraries/publications/University-Autonomy-in-Europe-2017.

Radó, Péter. "A felsőoktatás állami megszállásáról és annak következményeiről." *Beszélő*, May 22, 2015. http://beszelo.c3.hu/onlinecikk/a-felsooktatas-allami-megszallasarol-es-annak-kovetkezmenyeirol.

Readings, Bill. *The University in Ruins*. Cambridge: Harvard University Press, 1996.

Said, Edward W. "Identity, Authority and Freedom: The Potentate and the Traveler." In *The Future of Academic Freedom*, edited by Louis Menand, 214–29. Chicago: The University of Chicago Press, 1996.

Scholars at Risk. "Free to Think: Report of the Scholars at Risk Academic Freedom Monitoring Project," 2016. https://www.scholarsatrisk.org/wp-content/uploads/2016/11/Free_to_Think_2016.pdf.

Scholars at Risk Network. "Universities in a Dangerous World: Defending Higher Education Communities and Values," 2016. https://www.scholarsatrisk.org/wp-content/uploads/2016/10/SAR-2016-Global-Congress-Report.pdf.

Sen, Amartya. "Academic Freedom Becoming Alien Thought in India: Amartya Sen - Times of India." *The Times of India*, February 22, 2017. http://timesofindia.indiatimes.com/business/india-business/academic-freedom-becoming-alien-thought-in-india-amartya-sen/articleshow/57291168.cms.

Stanger, Allison. "Middlebury, My Divided Campus." *New York Times*, April 3, 2017.

———. "Understanding the Angry Mob at Middlebury That Gave Me a Concussion." *New York Times*, March 13, 2017.

Subaihi, Thamer Al. "Supporting Qatar on Social Media a Cybercrime, Says UAE Attorney General." *The National*, June 7, 2017. https://www.thenational.ae/uae/supporting-qatar-on-social-media-a-cybercrime-says-uae-attorney-general-1.31515.

Tierney, William, and Nidhi S. Sabharwal. "Debating Academic Freedom in India." *AAUP Journal of Academic Freedom* 7 (2016). https://www.aaup.org/JAF7/debating-academic-freedom-india#.WbD-bMhJZTM.

UNESCO. Recommendation concerning the Status of Higher-Education Teaching Personnel (1997). http://portal.unesco.org/en/ev.php-URL_ID=13144&URL_DO=DO_TOPIC&URL_SECTION=201.html.

Volokh, Eugene. "28 Harvard Law Professors Condemn Harvard's New Sexual Harassment Policy and Procedures." *The Washington Post*, October 15, 2014. https://www.washingtonpost.com/news/volokh-conspiracy/wp/2014/10/15/28-harvard-law-professors-condemn-harvards-new-sexual-harassment-policy-and-procedures/?utm_term=.e7a4631bd6c0.

Wiederstein, Michael. "Literatur Ist Rebellion." *Neue Züricher Zeitung*, July 7, 2016. https://www.nzz.ch/feuilleton/mario-vargas-llosa-im-gespraech-literatur-ist-rebellion-ld.104313.

Zha, Qiang, and Ruth Hayhoe. "The 'Beijing Consensus' and the Chinese Model of University Autonomy" 9, no. 1 (2014): 42–62.

Index